To Don Manning
Best Regards
Rose B. Lee

An American Dream

Rose Benté Lee

Morley ❖ Books

Copyright©Rose Benté Lee

All rights reserved. Except for use in a review, the reproduction or utilization of this work in any form or by any electronic, mechanical, or other means, now known or hereafter invented, including xerography, photocopying, and recording, and in any information storage or retrieval system is forbidden without permission of the publisher.

First Edition

ISBN 0-9660597-3-5
hardback only

Morley Books
1814 1/2 N Street, NW
Washington, DC 20036

To my husband Bill and our wonderful future together.

Acknowledgements

I want to thank the persons who helped me build "The House of Fine Fabrics" into a successful enterprise: Hisham Abu Zaggad ("Mr. Hank"), my nephew William "Willie" Leo Moeller, my niece Elisabeth Moeller, my niece Rosa Moeller Zyla, Agnes Skupin, Johann Kriss, Mr. Schwind, Eva Siegmann, Frieda Conner, Charles Conner, Jacquelin Dunn, Harold Evans, Leslie Nixon, my brother Leo Saemann and his wife Elisabeth Saemann, Edythe Soos, Fannie Schartenberg, and Katherina Sedelmeier, Shirley Smith, Hans & Lissy Weiss, James Michael von Stroebel, and Donald Landis.

For their ongoing moral support, I want to thank Marvin Weissberg, Father James Gould, Sister Eymard Gallagher, RSHM, Sister Majella M. Berg, RSHM, Louise Rhoads, Robert Neuland, Molly Cromwell, Col. Joseph and Theresa Brown, my nephew John Zyla and niece Lorraine Moeller.

I also want to express my thanks to the support of Robert Edward Lee, Michael Lee, Patricia Lee, the three children of Robert E. Lee, and Ray Bente's daughter, Yvonne Landis.

The law firm of Fletcher, Heald and Hildreth has been very generous with their help, including attorney Richard Hildreth, attorney Vincent Curtis, Jr., attorney Eugene M. Lawson, as well as attorney Donald Manning.

I would also like to acknowledge my other nieces and nephews, from Germany: Marianne Bickert, Gerda Bickert, Marianne Saemann, Karl & Ingrid Saemann, Udo Saemann, Elli & Werner Henniger, Imgard & Alfred Mattai; and in the United States: Rosalie & George Harvey, Ronald & Mary Lou Saemann.

Finally, I thank Deal Hudson for assisting me in writing this volume, and my husband William M. Ostapenko.

An American Dream

by Rose Benté Lee

Acknowledgements iv
Preface 1
Forward x

Chapter 1—Early Life 7
Chapter 2—Getting Started 25
Chapter 3—Growing Pains – Joys and Sorrows 43
Chapter 4—A Shock – And Growth 61
Chapter 5—New Beginning 75
Chapter 6—Gratitude and Giving 89
Chapter 7—Living Through the Arts 103
Chapter 8—A Healthy Community & Children 123
Chapter 9—Support for Education 141
Chapter 10—Giving Back to the Church 153
Chapter 11—Lessons from Life 171

Appendix 1—List of Philanthropies 182
Appendix 2—List of Honors and Awards 183
Appendix 3—15th Anniversary Poem by Robert E. Lee ..184

Forward

The story of the emigrant coming to America has always captured this nation's imagination. But too often these images stop with pictures of huddled figures gaping at the Statue of Liberty, or the long gray lines waiting to register at Ellis Island. Countless numbers of these families went on to realize the promises of liberty made at our nation's founding to all who would make their home on these shores.

From Italy and Ireland, Germany and Poland, from Russia, Spain, Mexico, and Vietnam, generations of emigrants have been woven together in a societal fabric of persons who can never forget the necessity of passing on the legacy of freedom and opportunity they themselves have received.

America is still a country of open arms. We must work to keep it that way. Some are urging us to close our shores to protect the wealth this country has created. To isolate ourselves during this time of abundance is to misunderstand the lessons of this country's history—we have prospered because we have invited all to work hard in a climate of freedom bolstered by faith.

It is my hope that this book will be a personal witness to the deep and often untapped resources of this country and the faith it was founded upon. May those who need encouragement to keep their dreams alive find it here.

Rose Benté Lee

Preface

My life is an American Dream. As a young girl I came to this country from Germany with no money, no obvious prospects, and no knowledge of the English language. But I understood that America was the land of opportunity—the land of the possible. Unlike in Germany, here there was the possibility of upward mobility. With hard work, vision, and a bit of luck, success was possible. Happiness, cultural enrichment, and intellectual growth were possible too. A young student with only a high school education might one day earn honorary degrees from some of our best colleges and universities. In America, dreams can come true.

Yet, in this land, success demands stewardship, service, and commitment to the community. If you are fortunate to have success in this wonderful country, there are strong expectations that you will give back to the community. This expectation is well-founded: Success has a price in terms of giving back to our churches, cultural organizations, educational institutions, nonprofit groups, and service projects.

The story of our country is also a history of philanthropy and remembering those who are less fortunate. Success has a steep price: Those who succeed financially, socially, politically, and culturally should always be conscious of their good fortune and of the need to become involved in efforts to make our communities healthier, more compassionate, environmentally safe, and less violent.

It is a matter of reciprocity—success is a gift. Those who succeed should be generous in return. This reciprocity is a vital, dynamic, and powerful force for good in our country. It can help to craft a better community for all of us.

For the vast majority of us, life is not easy. There are some days when life seems hopeless and cruel. But I have found that our courage, concern for others, and hope for a brighter future can help sustain us. For me, I found that courage, concern, and hope in the Catholic Church. In our village in Germany, the Church was a constant moral, intellectual, and spiritual guide. I welcomed her influence as a child, and I still depend upon the Church for guidance. I have not given up my freedom and remain stubbornly convinced that my life is my own responsibility. But the Church has been a good and comforting friend. I am so thankful for the presence of the Catholic Church in my own life.

Success does not come easily—for some it does not come at all. The deck may be heavily stacked against many of us, especially in some of our inner cities and rural areas. Many experience severe physical, emotional, or financial trauma, making it virtually impossible to live the life we would choose if circumstances were different. Success is the product of faith, hard work, discipline, financial prudence, and a bit of luck.

Success may bring personal satisfaction, peace of mind, purpose in life, and individual freedom. It is reaching your goals, whatever they are for each person. In America, more than any other country, each one of us has the chance—the opportunity—to reach our goals. We have the relative freedom to live our life for our own purposes and desires. This is a great country precisely because any person might achieve success.

My message is this: Everything being equal, there is a much greater chance that success, however you define it, will come to the person who chooses a profession that others value, who works hard, who strives for a high quality work product, who saves money, who has hope in the future, who develops and lives by a positive set of values, who reaches out to help others in the community, and who remembers the mutual dependency we have toward each other.

I write this book to document one person's encounter with the American Dream and to discuss the grave responsibilities that accompany it.

I dedicate this book to my family and friends. We have lived, worked, prayed, rejoiced, suffered, and laughed together. You have made my life rich beyond measure.

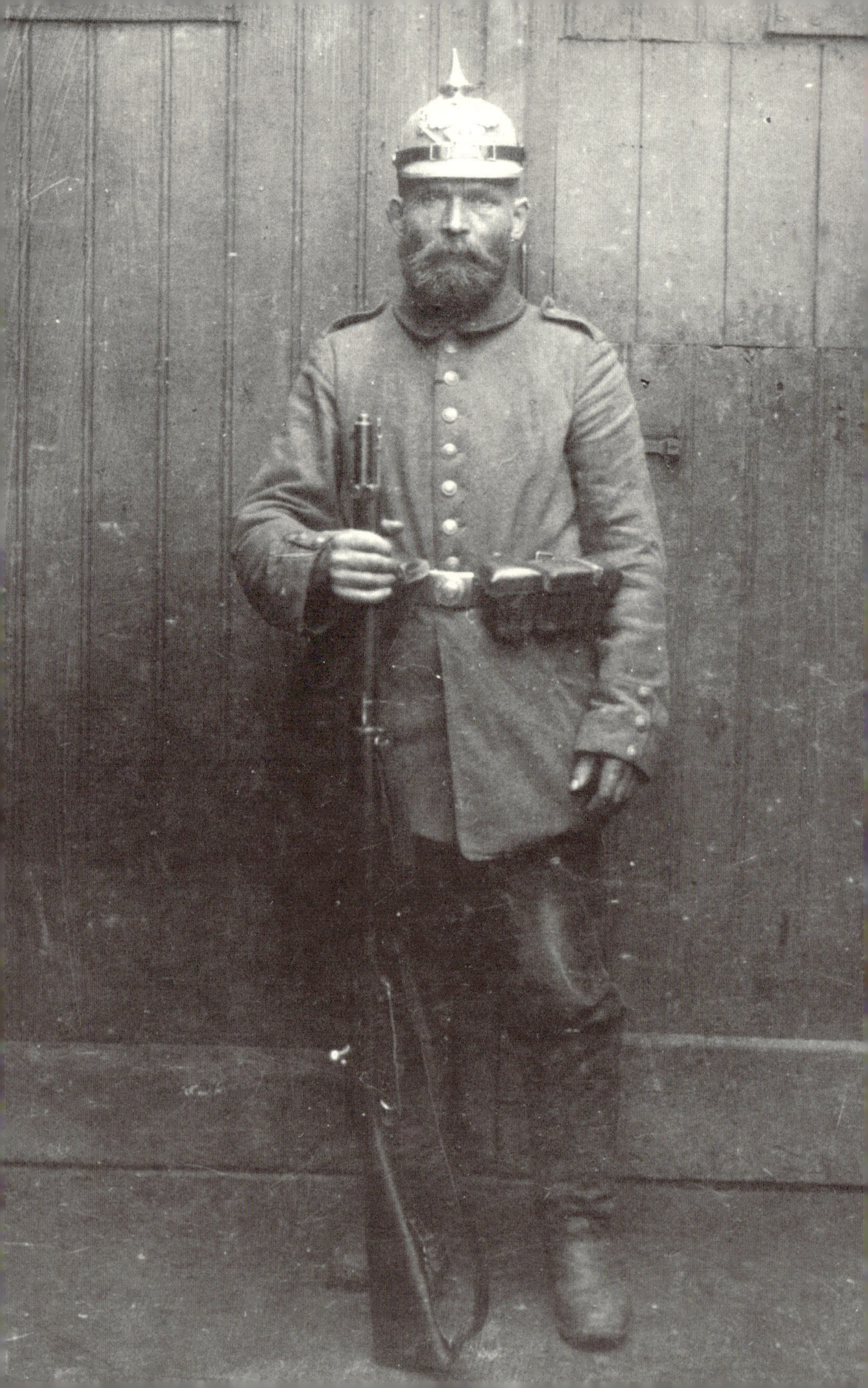

Chapter One

Early Life

When I returned to Germany in the late 40s, after the war, I visited my mother in my family's childhood home. I shall never forget my reaction to seeing that house again: "Good Lord," I remember thinking, "it's so small!"

I still remember that house: a two-story brick building on about two and one-half acres, surrounded by vegetable gardens and fruit trees. On the first floor was a formal parlor off the entrance hallway, with another family room and a big kitchen where my mother cooked the meals and ran the household. As a child, I remember it

Rose's father, Adam Joseph Saemann, in German Infantry uniform, 1916.

seemed like a big house, though I realize now that it was actually small—but that didn't matter to us as children—because my family was happy with each other's company. We didn't need big houses or lots of things to be happy and supportive of each other.

Papa, whose name was Adam Joseph Saemann, had passed away by then. He had been a builder, a respected trade in Germany. As a young man, he inherited a piece of land from his parents, in a town named Ruckers-Fulda near the old East and West German border, in the Wasser-Kuppe area. The town was, and still is, a place where the events of the twentieth century touched our lives only slightly. It was there that my father decided to put his trade to use for himself, by building a home and starting a family.

It happened that my father's friend and coworker, Joseph Becker, suggested one day that my father come to his home and meet his sister, who was visiting from her job as a personal attendant to Mrs. Opel. The Opels were a wealthy family that manufactured automobiles. My mother, worked for them in their home, becoming a trusted companion to his wife and children and almost a member of the family. Years later, the Opel family would visit Mama; sometimes they would bring us gifts. The coffee set, porcelain figures, and antiques they gave to us are still in our family.

It was love at first sight: Mama's regal bearing, culture,

The Saemann family home in Ruckers–Fulda, Germany.

beauty, and grace dazzled my father. At first, Mama was not so taken; she turned him down when he asked for a date. When he asked again, she refused him again. Not one to be put off—Papa was a very determined man—he proposed marriage; outraged, she turned him down once more.

But she gave in eventually, won over by his good nature, obvious love, and easy smile. They were very happy and very much in love all their lives. Papa was a quiet man, solid, with a mechanical eye and a determined nature. His one passion, besides my mother—whom he worshiped, calling her "my Anna-Maria"—was smoking his pipe. Mama was quite different: She was a beautiful woman, fashionable, and loved fine clothes and nice things. She was the more talkative of the pair and loved to laugh. She could also be as determined as Papa in loving her family and protecting her children. I don't recall them ever having an argument, not even about money or the children.

My childhood was harmonious and happy—our parents loved their children and provided for our material and spiritual needs, and we loved them in return. True spiritual love, my parents taught me, was really possible. In this and countless other ways, my parents, especially my mother, deeply influenced my life. They taught me to value hard work and to save money for the rough times of life. My mother, besides being beautiful, was the most patient, saintly woman I have ever known. She had a keen eye for her family and the events in their lives. She was kind but strong; she could be a stern disciplinarian but was never cruel. She taught me how to be a strong woman and a supportive wife.

My mother had learned how to be strong by living through hard circumstances. Papa had been wounded in the First World War, and four of his twelve children died in early childhood—a common occurrence at the time, but still heartbreaking to my parents. While Papa was at war, two of my siblings died within one week of each other. I still don't know how they made it through those trying times or how they lived with their grief at the loss of their little children. They didn't have time to grieve, for there was always work to be done.

Rose at age fourteen.

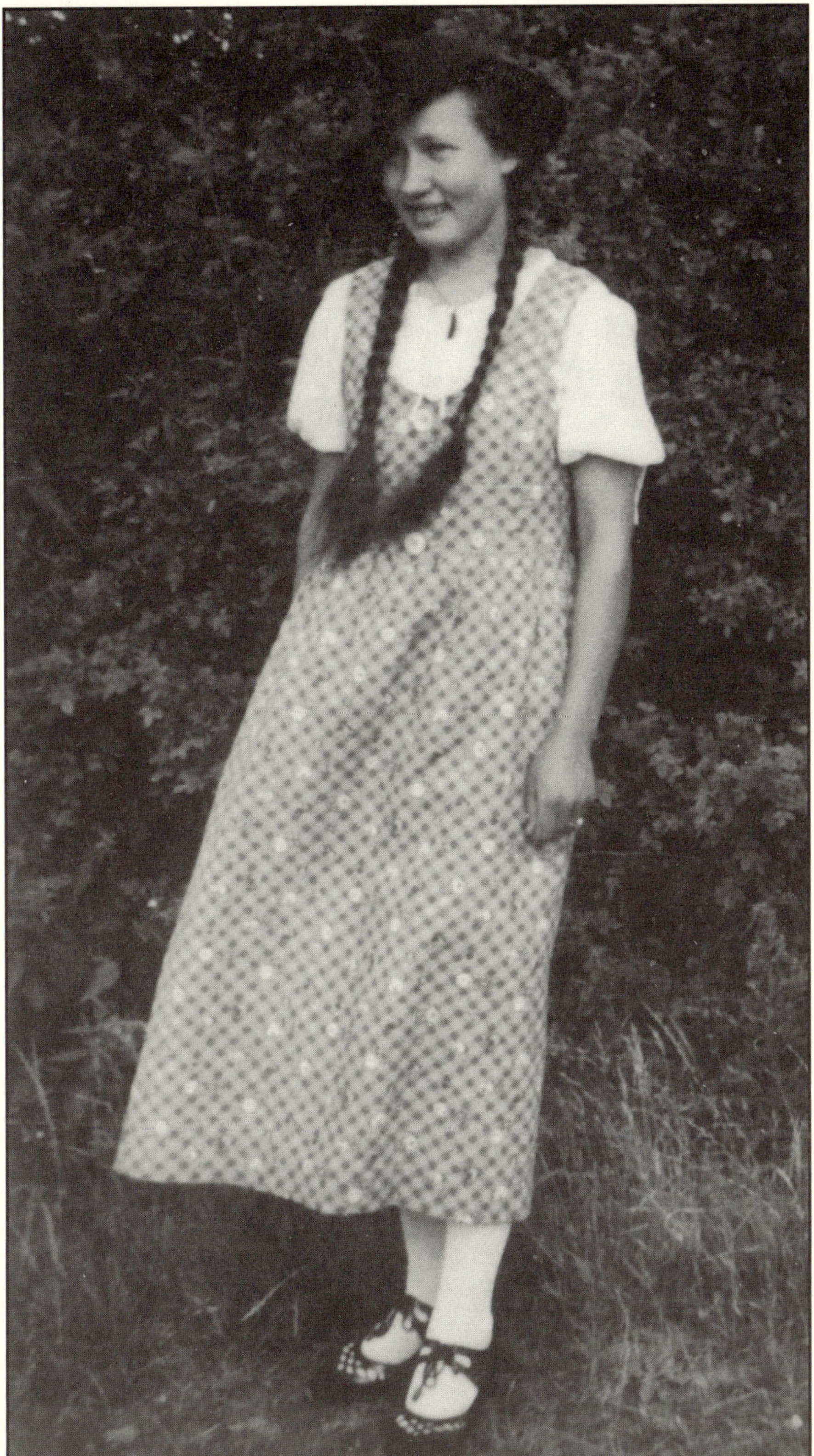

I remember Papa, Mama, and the happy childhood they gave us. We attended church every week, and afterward we would rest, perhaps take a walk, or read. Faith in God and Catholic devotions were always part of my life, which I believe gave my family a peace that all the troubles of growing up in Germany between the wars could not disrupt. Money and things, my parents taught me, aren't everything. Our family measured success in terms of hard work, honesty, and commitment. All of my siblings who lived to adulthood became businessmen or businesswomen, and all of us placed a high value on giving back to our community.

I was the baby of the family, and most of my brothers and sisters had left home by the time I was born. I looked a great deal like my mother, and as I grow older I realize that my personality is a great deal like hers. I remember my siblings would come home and bring me gifts: candy and small trinkets when I was young; later, perhaps a hat or a pocketbook. When I was very small, they would try to kiss me, so I would hide under my bed upstairs. My siblings were all hard workers and good people; they had been taught by Mama and Papa to work hard and save their money.

Anton was the oldest, much older than me, and I met him only a few times in my life, due to the great difference in our ages. He left home at a young age to live with my grandmother in Katzenberg, becoming, like Papa before him, an apprentice in the building trade—the traditional path into the construction and building trades. He eventually moved to Düsseldorf to start a construction company. After World War II, Anton was a leading figure in rebuilding Germany. He organized the people of Monheim, Cologne, and other towns to pick up the bricks and stones of destroyed buildings, clean them, and use them to build new homes, hospitals, and churches. Anton himself personally aided in the design and construction of a school, a church, and a hospital in Düsseldorf for the Catholic diocese there.

In 1954, Anton designed and built a beautiful, haunting statue of the Mother and Child, commemorating the women of Germany who had lost sons, brothers, fathers, and husbands in the war. The statue's sorrowful beauty reflected well Anton's own sorrow over the millions of lives lost on the front, and in the fire-bombings of cities like Monheim, Cologne, and Düsseldorf. Later in his life he was made a Knight of Malta for his many good works on behalf of the Catholic Church and the people of Germany—recognition of his role as a community leader in rebuilding the shattered cities of Germany. When he died, thousands attended his funeral from all across the country, as well as dignitaries from Monheim and Düsseldorf. Anton's example was always an inspiration to me; my siblings and I were all so proud of our oldest brother. Anton and his wife, Marichen, had two daughters, Marianne and Doris.

14 *An American Dream*

Augusta was the second oldest. She worked as a companion for the family of a rich merchant before marrying a local official, the assistant to the burgermeister in Ruckers. She lived with her husband and three children: son Willie, Rosa (named after me), and Elizabeth in a beautiful home, now a resort. Augusta's husband was killed on the Russian front during the war, and his remains are buried there in an unmarked grave for German soldiers. Her daughter Rosa came to the United States and lived with and worked for me for several years. Augusta herself came here in 1956, eventually living with me for six years and working in my business; in the meantime, her children joined us and also worked with us. We were very close.

After Augusta came my brother Herman, who was tall and handsome and studied engineering in Frankfurt. He would die at twenty-six of spinal meningitis after a high fever that lasted nine days, so I barely knew him. His death was a great shock to all of us, especially Mama, who took a long time to get over the sorrow.

The fourth sibling, Engelbert, was also in the war, and would be captured by the Russians. He spent several years in a prison camp, and after the war walked the hundreds of miles back to Fulda from Russia, surviving on food, drink, and clothing offered to him by the Russians—an almost unbelievable act of kindness from people whose lives had been nearly destroyed by the war. I remember his

Angela (age ten) and Rose (age six) at Angela's first communion.

stories of that long six weeks' journey very well; he would tell them to our family years afterward, always with great emotion. After he came home, Engelbert would make his living designing and building furniture and other items from wood. He was a fine craftsman—the best. He could make circular stairways that were a marvel, and his furniture and cabinets became known all over Germany. Eventually, he started his own factory, employing fifty people, and lived in Wasser-Kuppe for the rest of his life. Engelbert had three children—Karl, Elli, and Emgard.

Karl, too, was captured on the Russian front and made the long journey back to Fulda. He spent two months traveling by night and hiding by day in barns and forests, catching a little sleep. When he returned, he went into the building trade with my uncle in Frankfort; later he went to a university in Hanover and earned his doctorate in engineering, becoming quite wealthy. Karl was a talented, dynamic, and exact person; he had a gift for business, turning his small company in Hanover into a huge enterprise all across Germany.

Karl was also a student of architecture, becoming an expert in the history of German architecture and building design, and he would design and construct some of the most important buildings in the Hanover area, as well as highway tunnels for the autobahn. Politicians, businessmen, and community leaders, who respected him as an intelligent and humane man, sought Karl's advice and counsel. He died just recently, a great loss to the German building trade, and his memory is revered in Hanover as one of the most important community leaders of the last fifty years. He was also a loving husband and father of two children, Achim and Udo.

My brother Leo, who also recently passed away, broke with family tradition and became a baker. After an apprenticeship with a baker in Fulda, he was sponsored by my uncle to come to the United States, where he studied English in school during the day and worked in my uncle's bakery in Washington at night. Leo worked there until he opened his own bakery in Hyattsville, Maryland, the Supreme Bakery Shop. Leo became known through the Maryland suburbs as a master baker who could make remarkable pies, pastries, breads, and especially wedding cakes. Soon after, he had opened another shop in Washington, employing twenty bakers. Leo would write wonderful letters home, telling us of the opportunities available in the United States.

It was Leo's letters that made me decide to come to the United States. They were full of wonderful descriptions of this country, and he would often give us dollar bills when he came home to visit. His letters glowed with descriptions of how fair and free America was "Come here!" Leo would write. "In America, if you work hard and save, you can get somewhere. You can be a millionaire." Leo was right about America. When he died, he was a successful man. Leo and his wife, Elizabeth, had two children, Rosalie and Ronald.

My sister Angela was a designer. Her first husband was killed on the Russian front in World War II, but she has married again and has two lovely daughters, Marianne and Gerda. She still lives in Germany. She was a talented dressmaker and designer in Fulda, sharing her knowledge with me when I would apprentice with her after school; she inspired me to follow in her footsteps. I learned much of what would later make me a successful businesswoman from her—she had a wonderful eye for fabrics and clothing design, and she approached problems with Papa's steady eye. Angela was a role model for me, an inspiration. I can hardly hold a needle or see a spool of thread without thinking of her. She is my last living sibling, and we remain very close; I visit her every year in Frankfurt, where she lives. I owe her a great deal, for she gave me direction and purpose when I was a young girl.

Angela and I, the only siblings still alive, were part of a remarkable, talented family. All of us were successful in our chosen fields, because we absorbed the lessons that our parents taught us from a young age: Stay close to God, pray every day, love those around you, work hard, save, be kind to strangers, and love your family. Even as we scattered across Germany—and some of us crossed the Atlantic to the United States—we remained close and

Rose's Grandfather, Anselm Becker, age ninety-two, in Germany.

Rose Benté Lee   19

supportive of each other, and when we would gather back at home after the war, it was as if we had never left each other's side. I bless their memory every day and pray for them. I still love them deeply, and their love for me is a constant companion throughout my life. As the youngest, I was the recipient of their collective wisdom and kindness and have tried all my life to live up to the example of hard work and generosity that they had set.

I grew up like many German children, going to a private Catholic school, later spending two years at a finishing school in Fulda, and helping at the house. German school at the time was very strict. I remember they would sometimes hit us on the hand if we misbehaved; the boys would get even worse treatment—sometimes a paddling with a switch. The education, though, was very good, much better than in American schools. We were in the classroom from 8 a.m. to 3 p.m. and took very few vacations—just a week at Christmas and three weeks in the summer.

Teachers in those days were respected figures in the community. The female teachers never married, devoting their whole lives to educating children. In return, the community would support and provide for them. I was a good student, perhaps because I liked school so much. I was very shy, though, and that made me afraid to talk much in or out of class. As a young girl, my dream was to be a ballet dancer; I admired dancers for their grace and beautiful bearing.

In those days, you could only come to America if you had a family member to sponsor you, and you had to wait to receive an entrance visa. My sister Angela had applied to come to the United States and was ready to go when she met a boy and fell in love with him. She wanted to stay in Germany to marry him. Encouraged by Leo's letters and the stories I had heard from friends and family members who raved about the opportunities in America, I decided to take Angela's number and make the trip. I wrote to Leo, who bought me a ticket to New York, though I was able to pay him back with the first money I earned in the United States.

The Saemann family. Front row, left to right: Rose, Anna (mother), Adam Joseph (father), Angela. Back row: Augusta, Herman, Carl, Engelbert, Les, Anton.

Mama had to sign a letter giving me permission to go, because I was still a young woman, under eighteen. She did it with a heavy heart, because she was sad to see me go and hated to see her last child leave home, breaking up our happy family forever. But she signed the letter, because she knew that I would have a better life in America. She urged me to pray often and stay close to God and the Church, to work hard, and to be an upright young woman.

When it came time to go, to travel to the port—the first time I had ever even been out of Fulda—Mama came and kissed me with tears in her eyes. Papa was so sad to see his baby daughter leave for America that he could not make himself leave the garden to see me off. As I left, he stood around the corner, alone, and waved to me. It was the last time that I ever saw him, for he would pass away during the war, before I could come home.

And so I left for America and a new life.

Rose (left) and a shipboard companion.

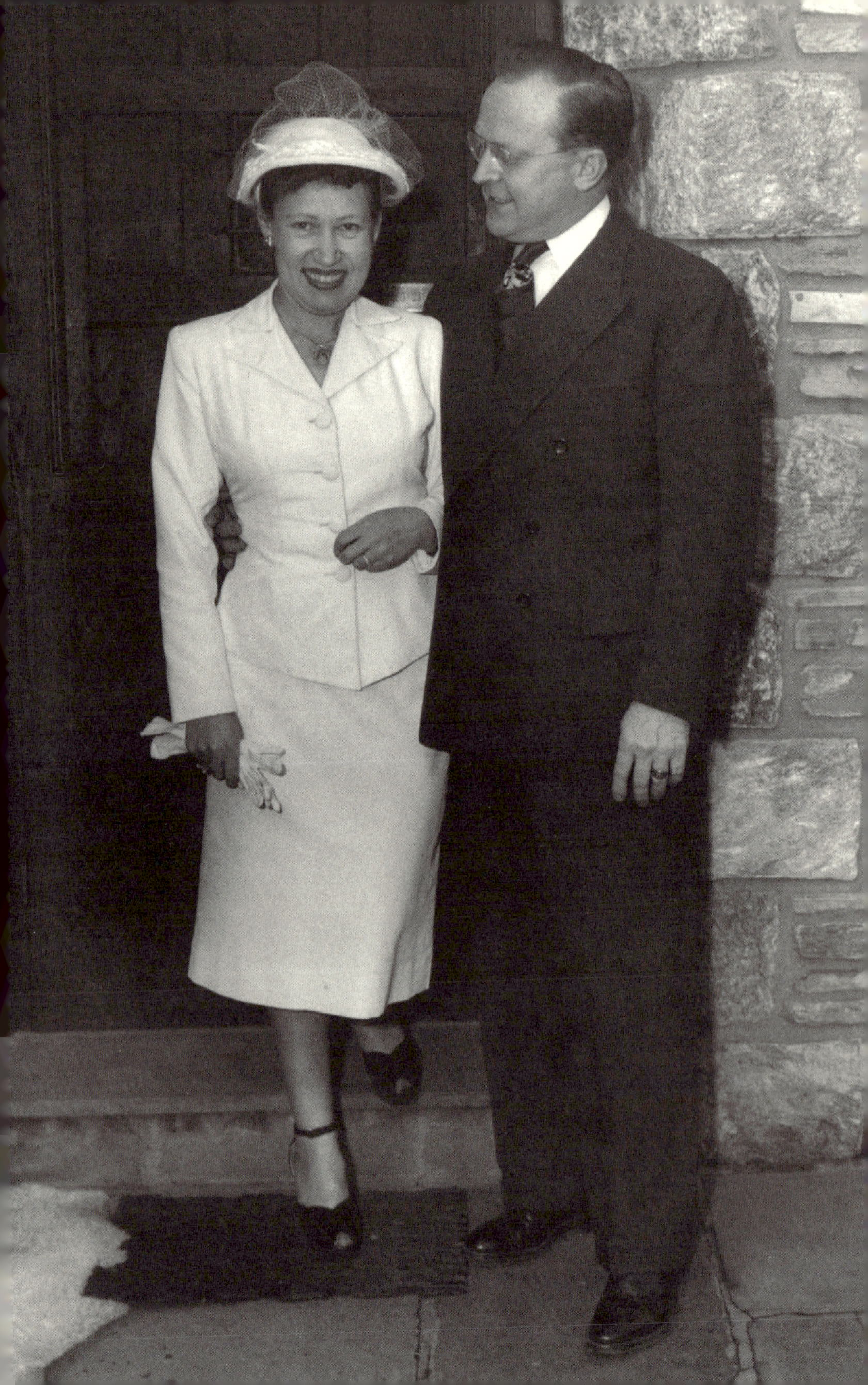

Chapter Two

Getting Started

The first thing I remember thinking about America was how busy everyone was and how hectic the pace was.

In Fulda the streets and houses were neat and clean, but in New York City, where I landed, everything was crowded and loud with automobile noises. I could barely believe that I had traded the trees of Fulda for the skyscrapers of New York. It was exciting, but a little frightening. To this day, I still don't how I had the courage to leave my home and go to a strange country. I would never do it today—but when you are young, everything seems possible.

Rose and first husband Ray Benté on their wedding day Dec. 29, 1950.

And everything did seem possible in America. Since coming to this country, making my life here, I have never really thought of myself as anything but American. Even as I struggled all those years to learn the language and customs of my adopted country, I was confident that America was the right place to be. Why? Perhaps it was Leo's glowing letters all those years, with his stories of how anyone who worked hard and saved could enrich his or her life in America. Perhaps I was simply restless to break out from our happy but uneventful life in Fulda. Or maybe it was just the excitability of being young. At the time, though, I didn't really think about why I wanted to leave, or all the apprehension of coming to a new place. I just went to America and expected the best.

Now, of course, I believe that it was the Holy Spirit guiding me to America because it was God's plan for me. Mama must have believed this, because she was such a person of prayer and strong faith that she would have never let me go unless she knew it was the will of God.

The trip to America on an ocean liner was exciting for a young woman who had never seen the sea. Every day I would look out over the wide ocean, wondering what was ahead, anxious for the journey to end and my new life to begin. Everything that I was seeing, in fact, was new—my trip through Germany to meet the ship was the first time I had ever been out of Fulda, the first time I ever got to see the rest of my native Germany.

Once I boarded that ship, I wouldn't be back for many years, almost a decade.

On the ship, I was "adopted" by two German ladies who were returning to their homes in New Jersey after a trip. I have always thought of them as my "guardian angels" on that journey. They would look out for me and make sure I didn't get into trouble on board. Later, I would write them at their homes in New Jersey. We exchanged Christmas cards and letters for years, and I would visit them at their homes on various occasions. They were my first American friends.

Leo came in his car and picked me up in New York, showing me around the city and stopping in interesting places during the trip down the East Coast to his home outside Washington, in Hyattsville, Maryland. For a young girl straight from a small town in Germany, the size and energy of these cities were awe-inspiring. Nothing in Fulda or the countryside of Ruckers could possibly prepare a person for Manhattan. Looking back, I realize that I must have seemed so young to Leo, even as I tried to act grown-up and worldly, but he was kindness itself and never laughed at me or patronized me. He took me into his home and gave me a start in America, and always encouraged me to follow my dreams, just as he had done in opening his own bakery. I will be forever grateful to him.

I went to an Americanization school for recent immigrants run by the government in Washington. By going

28   *An American Dream*

there, I could learn English as quickly as possible and earn my American citizenship. There were about twenty of us there, mostly girls, and our job was to spend the year learning English, so that eventually we could go to a local public school. I became friendly with many of the girls, two of them would be especially important to me: Marlies and Mathilda, whose homes in Washington I would visit several times. We would often go out to have fun, and had wonderful time at social events, dances, and parties at the USO and the Red Cross. I have remained interested in the Red Cross to this day, participating in many of their activities.

It was a wonderful time in my life, but there were many struggles. Getting to the Americanization school was hard: an hour from Hyattsville by streetcar each way—tiring on any day, but especially difficult in the winter. And learning the language, of course, was far from easy. The first sentence taught, "This is a chair," the teacher said pointing to the seats we were sitting in. Learning English was a struggle; every day I would learn new words and repeat them, over and over. Of course, there were times when I made mistakes. I remember Leo's wife sending me to the drugstore to buy her a bottle of ink. I repeated over and over again the sentence, "I want a bottle of ink," which I was supposed to say to the clerk at the store. I could say it perfectly all the way down the block, but when I got to the store, it just disappeared from my mind. I'll always remember standing in front of the

Rose and her brother Leo at his home in 1951.

clerk, embarrassed, trying to stammer out the forgotten sentence I thought I had committed to memory. I had to walk back to our apartment and have my sister-in-law write it down. Fortunately, Hyattsville—where I was living with Leo at the time—was a small town, and everyone knew that I was learning English. They were all very kind. People are still very kind, because sometimes I still make mistakes with English, even after all these years.

Eventually, after two years, I knew English well enough to leave the Americanization school and get a job—I had definitely had enough of the trip downtown. Marlies helped me to find a job with the Singer Sewing Machine Co. in downtown Washington. There I would use the skills that my sister Angela had taught me back in Fulda.

I quickly established myself as a competent and dedicated worker, and Singer had made me an instructor, teaching other women how to sew and use Singer sewing machines. It was at Singer that I got my first education in business, and working there only deepened my love of sewing and fabrics. I have always been fascinated by clothes and fashions—it came from Mama, who always dressed beautifully despite being financially limited. She was a beautiful woman, and she loved to wear beautiful things. I take after her—to this day I check all the new designer lines as they come out of New York and read all the latest fashion magazines.

Eventually, I had saved enough money to pay Leo back for the ticket to America, and decided to move into a little place of my own. Marlies had a friend who lived in a boarding house for young ladies run by a German family on Connecticut Avenue and L Street, and she helped me find a room there. They were good people, very kind, and they kept a good eye on us, but they were very strict. The curfew at the house was early, and if you wanted to meet your boyfriend, you had to meet him in the front hallway, where there were sure to be a few "accidental" interruptions by members of the family.

But it was a wonderful time to be a young girl in Washington, despite that my new homeland was at war with my native country. The soldiers and sailors would come home on leave, and we girls who lived in the house would take the bus to dances at the USO or join other groups in Washington for parties. The girls in the house were all my good friends; when I look at the pictures from those days, I'm struck by how young we all were, though we thought of ourselves as very modern and sophisticated.

I dated a few of the soldiers and officers, but never seriously. There were too many barriers between me and many of the boys I met during the war, barriers of language, culture, and interests, though I never experienced any discrimination as a German native while America was fighting Germany in the Second World War.

I grieved for what was happening in Germany, worried for my family, especially my brothers, whom I knew were fighting on the front, though there was no communication between my family and me during the war—mail couldn't be sent between Germany and the United States. Since the two countries were at war with each other, I was especially sad to see the destruction that my native countrymen were subjected to by the Nazi leaders,

but I always supported America in the war, and people understood my patriotism and love for my adopted country. In fact, one of the young soldiers wanted me to marry him and move to Nebraska, even though I couldn't have picked Nebraska out on the map. I turned him down.

Soon, though, I met Ray Benté, who was trained as an accountant and who was the manager at the Singer Sewing Machine Co. We first met at a Christmas party given by the company; I was attracted to him at once. He was tall and handsome, friendly and charming, the sort of person the entire room gravitated toward. I liked him as soon as we met, especially after I found out that he was a fantastic dancer. A few years later, we started dating. Ray was a wonderful man, and like many easygoing, likeable people, he was a salesman's salesman. He always wore a white shirt and tie, he smoked a pipe, and his manner put you right at ease. We became very serious about each other, and soon decided to be married.

Both of us had the same dream: to establish our own company, to be our own boss. We both wanted to open a retail business, but America was in the middle of World War II, so fabrics, appliances, and sewing materials were in short supply, since everything was being used for the war effort. Besides, neither of us had any money, though I had an iron, an ironing board, a portable Singer sewing machine, and an antique sewing machine that Ray would convert to an electric machine. (I still use that machine in

Rose working for the Red Cross in 1949.

my home today.) But we kept dreaming and planning, and I kept my eye on a little shop on Connecticut Avenue that was available for rent near my room in the rooming house. I tried to save money, both from my meager salary and some alteration work I did on the side for a dressmaker whose shop was located underneath the old Scholl's Cafeteria.

Finally, we made the leap: It was scary, but exhilarating, to be on our own. We rented that little shop on L Street and Connecticut Avenue near the White House from the Rizick family. At $200 a month, this little store, we hoped, would catch the lunch trade of office workers who might need dresses and shirts repaired and altered. Now, that whole area of Washington is full of fifteen-story office buildings housing lawyers, lobbyists, and brokerages, but at that time it was all small shops and houses, with a few hotels like the Mayflower across the avenue for congressmen and official visitors. It is amazing to think how much Washington has changed in just a short time.

After we got married, Ray and I rented a little one-bedroom apartment on New Hampshire Avenue, but for all intents and purposes we lived at the shop, working sixty- and seventy-hour weeks. (Even our honeymoon was only one day, spent at home—we didn't have the money for even one night out.) Before we started the business, I had saved $800 from my salary and got a loan on my life insurance policy for another $250; Ray sold his

Rose (far right) with two friends from the Singer Sewing Company

car. We had to pay for everything in cash because we had no credit. Ray built the shelves that we used to display our merchandise. We spent a lot of time researching various fabrics and supplies to find what we liked at the cheapest possible prices. There was no room for error: We didn't have the money to make mistakes. So we hung our sign on the front door: "The Sewing Shop."

After six months in operation, we hired a part-time employee, Mrs. Harris. She and I did alterations upstairs; I taught sewing classes in the evening for women needing to learn a skill; Ray worked in the damp basement, repairing sewing machines and appliances because people could not get any new equipment. We were open for business. Ray and I smiled at the realization of our dreams—and got to work, because we knew if we were going to make it, we had to work hard for long hours.

We did. We had no money for advertising, so our business grew by word of mouth, which meant we had to work hard enough so as to impress each customer that he or she would tell a friend. Fourteen-hour days were not unusual for Ray and me, and there were times when we barely had the money to pay the rent on the shop and buy food. Every Monday through Sunday, we would be in by 6 a.m. and we didn't close until 6:30 p.m. But even then we did not go home—at night, we had to prepare for the next day, or I had to teach sewing classes in the back of the shop and Ray would repair sewing machines in the basement, so our lights would still be burning at 11 p.m. or every midnight. On Sundays, we were closed to the public, but that was the time we used to catch up on sewing, do the books, and clean the store. It was hard work, and we really struggled; once, in fact, a friend was kind enough to loan us the money to pay our rent, because we weren't going to make it that month. We allowed ourselves no frills: no eating out, no expensive clothes, no vacations. Every dime we made we put back into the business.

Those were hard times, and sometimes it seemed as if we wouldn't make it, but little by little we built a reputation as a place where you could get quality products and services at reasonable prices. In fact, the first day we took in $50, which seemed like a fortune to us at the time! We did everything in that little shop: Ray and I cleaned the floors, washed the windows, repaired the shelves, and made signs and price stickers ourselves. Each of us brought different but complementary strengths to the business. Ray was a fantastic salesman and a smart businessman; he kept the books and I kept my eye out for fabrics and supplies that were reasonably priced—a "must" for us at the beginning when we had no credit and paid for everything COD. I had a good eye for quality and a sense of what would come in and out of style. To this day, I only have to feel a fabric for just a moment to tell you what it's made of and whether it's good quality or not.

We were helped by our fortuitous timing. The war was coming to an end just as we set up The Sewing Shop, and women's styles, which had tended toward short skirts, suddenly went longer. Women in Washington, of course, wanted to keep up with the fashions, but no one had any money to buy new dresses. So we did a lot of business in lengthening and modifying dresses and skirts for the women who worked downtown, adding fabric to make an old piece of clothing look new. When people had more money, they would come to me to design and sew their new wardrobe.

We were also helped by our location, which was convenient to the downtown firms and government offices, and we were helped by Washington itself, which was—and is—an image-conscious town. It is important—in fact, vital—that anyone starting out in business determine where the market is and tailor his business strategy to attract that customer. From my time at the Singer Sewing Machine Co., while sewing and studying textile fashion from various sources, I understood that the men and women in Washington like quality fabrics and well-cut clothing. It is not a town with the flair of New York or other large cities, but it is a place where people like to appear successful, which means dressing in a way that looks expensive. Washingtonians look for high-quality, durable, sophisticated fashion. I realized this and looked specifically for those kinds of fabrics on my buying trips to New York City and other places. I also stocked a variety of silks and more expensive fabrics to serve the Embassy Row diplomats who began to come to our shops, looking for me to design and make a one-of-a-kind cocktail or formal dress for official events. Ours was the only shop of its kind in Washington, and we could make a suit or repair a dress faster and better than any other shop.

By the end of that first year, we had four girls working for us, that few only because we could not fit any more people into the small space! Ray took care of the front, selling fabrics and notions, and at night continued to repair sewing machines and appliances. I sewed in the

Ray Benté and nephew William Moeller at Connecticut Ave. store.

back, fitting dresses and taking orders, and managed the girls. I also continued to teach sewing in the evenings, though more and more of my time was being taken up by managing the business—purchasing materials, working on the books, and designing dresses.

Soon Ray and I had the money to get a nice one-bedroom apartment up on Connecticut Avenue, near the Uptown Theatre. At this time my niece Rosa came over from Europe and joined Ray and I in our apartment. The business was growing day by day, and soon we felt confident enough to open a second shop in Suitland, Maryland. Our hard work was paying off, and our dreams were beginning to come true. I felt things could get better, and they did. But there were still rough times ahead.

Rose and Ray at the Lotus Club, Washington D.C., 1952.

Rose Benté Lee   41

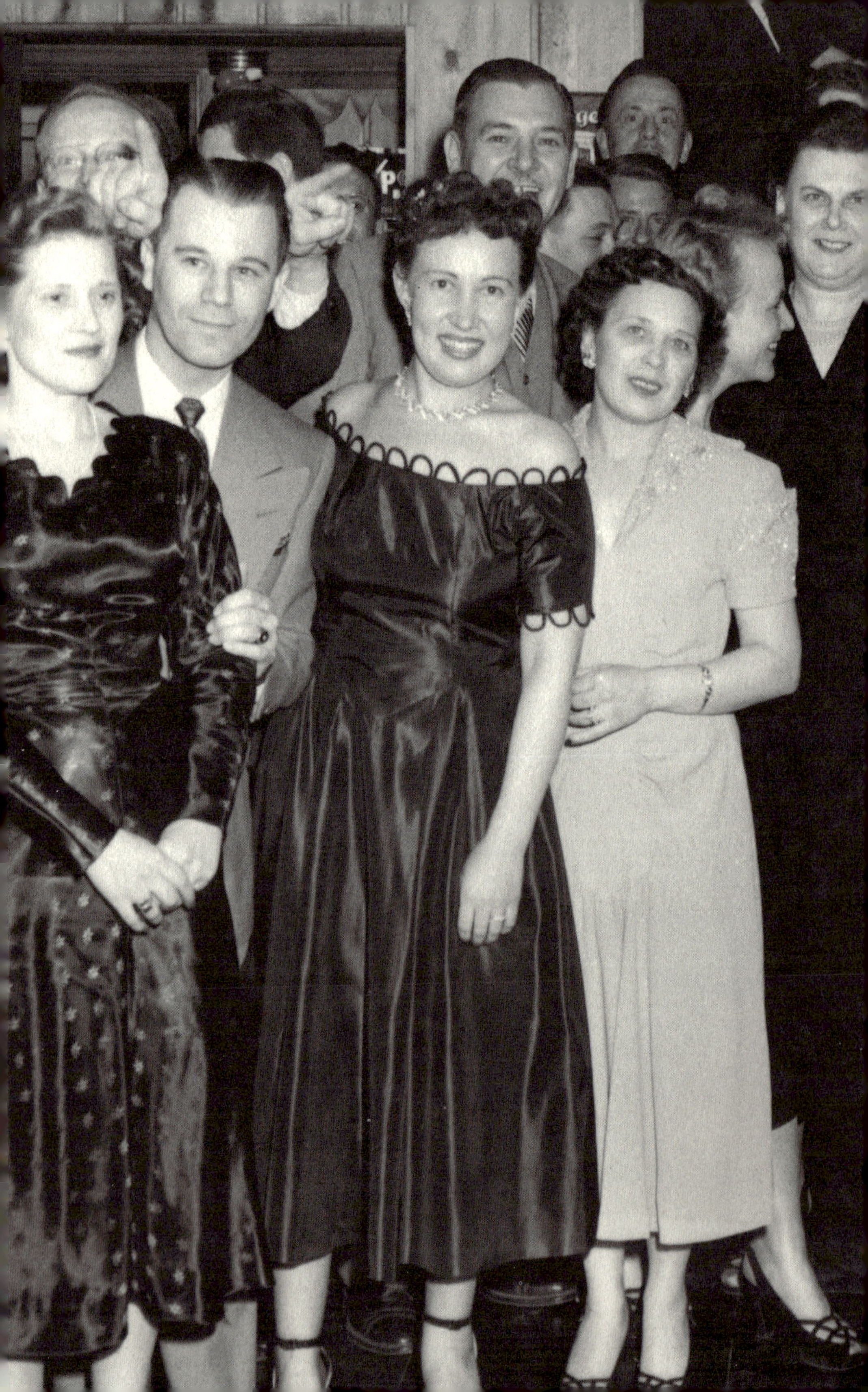

Chapter Three

Growing Pains – Joys and Sorrows

After a year in business, we could catch our breath a little. The business was growing daily, and we were beginning to be noticed around the nation's capital as the best place to go for quality sewing and reasonably priced material.

We had started by catering to the secretaries and office workers downtown, offering them high-quality service—a necessity if you were going to get ahead in Washington—at prices that a young government employee on a budget could afford. We never abandoned those

Rose (center) and friends at a party at brother Leo's home, 1951.

customers, but as we grew, we began to be patronized by members of the elite social set in Washington.

Most of the first ladies came into our shop, including Jackie Kennedy, Ladybird Johnson, and Pat Nixon, as did the presidents' own tailors. We offered these dignitaries comfortable shopping, discretion, and unparalleled service. It was easy to come in and look around, and everyone who came through our door was treated with respect and courtesy, regardless of position. We didn't hustle people through or make snap judgments, because every customer was important to us and we let them know it. Ray instilled the right attitude in every seamstress and salesperson in the shop, letting them know the difference between "What do you want?" and "How can I help you?"—sometimes pretty sharply, if he felt it was necessary.

Ray was such a good man; he would always take the sting out later by helping those employees he reprimanded, perhaps having coffee with them or just showing them some extra encouragement. He was committed to the business and committed to customer service, but he never forgot that the people he worked with were still human beings deserving of respect. Our employees worked hard, but we were all like a family, and Ray made sure everyone felt themselves a part of that family.

We started to do more high-level designing, making dresses for diplomats' wives that would be worn to White House parties and Embassy Row cultural events. We had to be prepared to satisfy the woman looking for fabric to make an impressive evening dress, as well as fabrics for less formal occasions. We quickly adjusted to fit the needs of this sort of customer, who was looking to have her dress discussed the next morning in the *Washington Post* Style section. Our shop began to buzz with customers discussing "that party at the White House next week" or "cocktails at an embassy." We were thrilled and very thankful for these customers, but never let it go to our heads—the downtown crowd was still our bread and butter, our most loyal customers.

Soon we had outgrown our location and moved to a new space on Connecticut Avenue. The Sewing Shop, which became "The House of Fine Fabrics," was being noticed as a Washington success story. We also began to advertise in local papers and the *Washington Post* for the first time: "Complete line of fabrics, patterns, notions, trimmings, buttons—Famous patterns from designers all over the world!" Ray and I were glad to be able to reach a wider audience, and the advertising paid off as the number of customers in our stores increased.

At this stage of my developing business, it became imperative that I acquire trustworthy, honest, reliable help who would unstintingly support me and give me unquestioning loyalty in my efforts. Naturally, I turned to my family in Germany, where I was able to find the kind of help that I needed.

FABRICS

SUITLAND BRANCH ONLY!
New Permanent Drapery-Slipcover Dept.

50,000 Yds. of All First Quality
ANTIQUE SATINS—PRINTS—SOLIDS
COTTONS—FORTISANS

from 1.98 to 4.98

$1.00 yd.

DRESS FABRIC SALE
BOTH STORES

Woolens .... 54" wide **$1.88**
Corduroys .... Reg. $1.19 **88¢**
French Woolens **$4.98 to $5.98**

USED BY THESE FAMOUS DESIGNERS

Jacques Heim		Jean Patou
Jean Desses	Jacques Griffe	Guy Laroche
Gris Pierre Cardin	Nina Ricci	Jeane Lanvin
Givenchy	Balenciaga	Pierre Balmin

for the Holiday Season
Domestic & Imported

BROCADES From **$1.49 to $19.95**

IMITATION FUR FABRICS — PERSIAN LAMB LEOPARD BROADTAIL CHINCHILLA

The Sewing Shop

1122A CONNECTICUT AVE., N.W.
OPPOSITE MAYFLOWER HOTEL
NA. 8-9857

4634 SUITLAND RD., S.E., SUITLAND, MD.
OPPOSITE CENSUS BUREAU
RE. 6-1818

My sister Augusta, who was a widow, had three children, William, Rosa, and Elizabeth. They had the capabilities that I needed, and were of the age that would be of help to me. At this point in time, the war with Germany had been concluded, and the country was economically destitute, its population to a large degree unemployed.

My family was in dire straits and in need of economic assistance. I, of course, realized that I could be of help to my family and they could in turn be of great help to me in my business's future. Therefore I arranged to have my family join me in the United States.

In due time my family arrived, and in short order were employed in my business. They adjusted quickly and to a large degree were successful in the management of individual stores. My niece Rosa was the manager of the Suitland store and the Connecticut Avenue store, where her performance was outstanding. My nephew William and niece Elizabeth also performed in an outstanding manner in their respective assignments well into the future. William subsequently became the manager of three successful stores.

My hopes and expectations from my family were more than adequately fulfilled beyond my fondest dreams, and contributed most importantly to the ultimate success of my business.

Before too long we had outgrown even our new location, and moved again on Connecticut Avenue next door

Washington Post advertisement for the Suitland Branch.

to a larger space. Our flagship downtown store was located permanently on Connecticut Avenue across from the majestic Mayflower Hotel. The Mayflower is the oldest, most prestigious hotel in Washington—it was where dignitaries, high-level, wealthy visitors would stay when they came to the nation's capital. Our location right across the street was a sign that we had made it. I had rented extra office space in which to do the books and paperwork associated with our expanding business, and where I conducted business, purchasing inventory and merchandise from all over the world.

Another sure sign that we had become a success in the urbane, upscale world of Washington was the attention we got from Garfinckle's. Garfinckle's was a legend in Washington—it still is a legend among older Washingtonians, years after the store was forced to go out of business. Garfinckle's sold dresses off the rack. Impressed by our growing clientele and by the quality of our work, Garfinckle's eventually asked us to take over a great portion of its alteration needs. This was extraordinary for the most high-level shop in Washington to do, and we were extremely flattered by the compliment. In fact, Mrs. Messinger, the fashion coordinator for the store, even came to me to make some of her clothes. On one occasion, I made her an Easter outfit of three layers of blue taffeta which was featured in the *Washington Post*.

With our financial situation improving, Ray and I

decided to move out of our apartment to a new home in suburban Virginia, across the river in Arlington.

Our business was growing, and Ray and I soon felt confident enough to open new stores. We had always hoped to do this, knowing that the key to a successful operation was maximizing our potential customer base—and the only way to do that was to expand to as many locations as possible. The timing was right, we knew. The store was doing an expanding business, but the move to the suburbs had begun in earnest in Washington. Many government agencies had opened branch offices in Maryland and Virginia, and new developments were springing up in the counties ringing the District of Columbia. These developments were full of mothers with families, and I knew that many of them would appreciate the convenience of having a full-service shop with fabrics, patterns, and notions nearby. Besides that, in each of these developments a new kind of shopping area was springing up—the shopping center, which put a variety of stores right next to each other so that a busy suburban mother could do all her errands in one trip. All these events came together at once, and Ray and I knew that the time had come to expand.

But where to go? One of our regular customers was the vice president of a new shopping center in Seven Corners, at the intersection of Routes 50 and 7 in suburban Virginia. "You've got to come to Seven Corners," she told us, "we have traffic all day long at the new center!" We looked at the location, and she was right about the traffic—but there were no stores open that would be big enough. We kept the location in mind and went elsewhere.

We also decided to expand our product line. In the early days of The Sewing Shop, we couldn't stock a lot of fabric for sale, only what we used to make dresses—remember, we had no credit and paid cash for everything. It was important to keep overhead costs down and not have too much of our money tied up in inventory. But now that we were doing more business, more and more of our customers wanted us to sell fabric so that they could make their own clothes at home. We thought, why not? So we began to buy fabrics to sell to our customers, which of course required more floor space and more sales associates. But it also required a new name, to reflect the fact that fabric sales more and more became the central product that we offered to customers. "The House of Fine Fabrics," Ray and I decided, reflected both our reputation as a place where you would get respectful, attentive service and high-quality products.

We had found the name that would make us successful, we felt. I was excited for the future.

But before success came, we had to expand our operation. After looking at a variety of locations around the area, Ray and I settled on a new shopping center in Suitland, Maryland. The real estate agent assured us

"Bishop Method" sewing class in the basement of the Suitland Store.

that the location received a lot of traffic during the day, and I noticed that the center was across the street from a new branch office of the U.S. Census Bureau. The parking lot full of shining cars convinced me that the people in the surrounding buildings, plus mothers visiting the shopping center in the middle of the day, would make the new store as much a success as the Connecticut Avenue store.

As it turned out, we were wrong. The people from the Census Bureau wouldn't cross the street on their lunch break, and the mothers didn't come in the numbers that we needed to make the store a success. Not the success we were hoping for—but it was a valuable lesson in doing your homework on an area before you moved, a lesson we learned.

We added an interior decorating department, which included decorating and outfitting high-ranking military officers' private residences, as well as the military officers' clubs located at Andrews Air Force Base and the Bolling Air Force Base.

The lower levels of the Suitland store were converted to sewing classes, training students, which included housewives as well as younger trainees, in the "Bishop method" of sewing.

In addition, space was made available for warehousing materials and supplies for the other "House of Fine Fabrics" stores. Eventually, the entire Suitland store operation became a highly successful location.

When we started the business, I would go on buying trips to New York, looking for fabrics and other supplies. I always loved those trips. As the business began to grow, though, the fabric companies began to come to me, not only from New York, but from Paris, Milan, Switzerland,

and as far away as Japan, once that nation began to produce the popular polyester blends—a sure sign that we were a growing success. In buying a fabric, I looked for two things: pattern and quality. I would always keep up with the fashion lines coming out every spring and fall, taking my cue as to what would be popular from the most stylish designers, such as Holstein, Pierre Cardin, and others. You had to have products that people wanted to buy, because they had many options and would go elsewhere to make their purchases if you did not give them a reason to stay. I also looked for quality. I felt that the products offered for sale in my store were a direct reflection of me, a direct reflection of my good taste (or lack of it), and I worked to instill that sense in our employees. I would always enjoy the compliments: "Rose, I love this printed Swiss cotton and chiffon," or, "Where did you find this lovely red Swiss silk?" Of course, every purchase carries an element of risk, and sometimes we would make the wrong choice.

The keys were quality and keeping prospective customers in mind with each purchase. I was sure that our clientele in status-conscious Washington would buy something that was a little more expensive if they thought they were getting higher quality, rather than buy a cheaply made alternative. I shopped for fabrics the same way that I expected my customers would—looking for the best quality at the least expensive price. I would feel the fabric, examining the weave and the fibers, and if I only found one bolt from a manufacturer that I liked, I would buy just that one bolt, even though I could have saved money by buying several lower-quality fabrics alongside it for a bulk discount.

Also important was customer feedback. Now, the most immediate feedback is, of course, the sales receipts—what the customers don't like, they won't buy. But I have always thought that it is important for a retail operation to get personal comments from customers to guide the buying process. Nothing can substitute for face-to-face comments and reactions from the people who buy your products. And to get those face-to-face comments, you have to have people on the sales floor at all times, asking customers their opinions and getting their reactions to various fabrics. You want to know why they purchased this fabric over that one; you want to discuss their needs and their preferences when they make their purchasing decisions.

To boil it down to an old cliché, the customer is always right, because we are trying to meet the needs of the customer. The customer is always smarter than you; if you let yourself think you know more than the customers, they will repay you by taking their dollars—and their loyalty, a commodity you can not put a price on—to another store. We serve our clients, they do not serve us. "The House of Fine Fabrics" would never have been successful if we felt that the clients were lucky to have us. Instead, we were lucky to have them.

Our first expansion to Suitland had not gone as well as we had hoped, so we were determined to make new locations successful. Originally, we had hoped to expand to Seven Corners, but as I said, the mall had no openings large enough. When we were ready to open our third store, though, a spot had come open. We jumped at the opportunity, being impressed by the quality of the stores in that shopping center and the make-up of the community around it. This time, we did it right: Seven Corners was a wildly successful store for "The House of Fine Fabrics," one of the best in the chain that we would eventually open. From Seven Corners, we opened stores at a rapid pace in Chevy Chase, White Oak, Landover, and many other locations in Maryland and Virginia.

Like all stores in the growing chain, the Connecticut Ave. store featured fabrics selected for the specific needs of the neighborhood's customers.

We were growing, but we were also small enough to keep a close eye on all our stores. We always looked for the same things at any location we were considering: whether there was enough midday foot traffic (after we expanded to the suburbs, noon remained the busiest time in all our stores, as employees from local businesses would drop off things to be altered or pick up a few yards of fabric), whether there were enough stores in the shopping center to attract the people needed to sustain the business, and whether there were enough mothers looking for good fabrics in the vicinity.

We also individualized our purchases to reflect the makeup of the area around each of the stores. For example, our store in Chevy Chase—a wealthy Maryland suburb where many of the people in the vicinity were high-powered attorneys, lobbyists, or bureaucrats in downtown Washington—carried more of our high-end designer fabrics than many other stores. Our sales clerks would notify our customers regarding these fabrics, and they subsequently would call their dressmakers, who would also come in and help select these fabrics, and the dressmakers would them make their gorgeous cocktail dresses and well-tailored suits.

Seven Corners, though, had a higher percentage of stay-at-home moms who wanted a wide selection of durable fabrics and notions for use in making clothes for their children. These distinctions, which helped to make each of our stores highly successful, were the product of spending a lot of time studying the area and its inhabitants and listening to our customers on the sales floor. In every store in our rapidly growing chain, though, you could also get a great deal on quality fabrics and always fantastic customer service.

Our growing group of stores also required Ray and I to shift our job descriptions just a little. No longer could we personally oversee every detail in every store; we had to find and hire honest, hardworking managers who shared our values and our sense of customer service. We spent more and more time involved in the paperwork of running a business—receipts, ledgers, purchasing orders, and the like. I taught myself bookkeeping and some basic accounting, and I had to learn how to calculate taxes from a paycheck, assign a cash value to benefits, and all the other little details of managing employees. But I never let these details get me too far from my first love: interacting with customers, managing the stores themselves, overseeing the alterations, and buying the fabrics.

We had stores at all points of the Beltway, the highway that rings Washington, and I began to build up the miles on my car driving to each of the stores at least once a week to overlook operations and keep our salespeople on their toes. The managers at "The House of Fine Fabrics" were like a family; many of my employees ended up being with me twenty years or more. We expected much from them, but we were loyal and generous to our employees. Never in all my time as a business owner did I ever encounter a labor dispute. The managers knew we would always treat them well, and they repaid us with their hard work and devotion.

There were many people who were important to the success of our business, one of whom was "Mr. Hank," Hisham Abu Zayyad, who worked as a regional manager and then as vice president from 1968-1978. I had hired "Mr. Hank," who became my right-hand man, helping me in many ways: in the selection of merchandise, overseeing the efficiency in our daily operations, and especially in the challenging task of opening new stores for our expanding business.

There was Agnes Skupin, who worked for more than thirty years in management, and Charles Connor, who worked on weekends remodeling our stores and accomplishing other related support work.

As I mentioned earlier, my nephew Bill Moeller managed many of our stores and continued to work after 1978. My niece Rose (Zyla), who managed the Suitland store at this time, and her sister Elizabeth were an indispensable part of our success.

Every day brought us closer and closer to our dreams, and Ray and I were happy and satisfied with our life together. "The House of Fine Fabrics" was growing daily, expanding to new locations, and gaining new customers who appreciated what we had to offer in the way of price and quality.

Rose and Ray working at the second store on Connecticut Ave.

All this time, though, my mind kept returning to Germany, and the difficult times that my native country was being forced to endure after the war. I had never been able to communicate with my family during the war, and it was a great shock to me when I found out that Papa had passed away. There were always severe shortages of food and medicine, and Ray and I tried to help out as much as we could during that time, sending over money, clothes, canned food, thread and fabric, anything we could to Mama, Augusta, and Angela. In that time, we were their lifeline. I was always sad to hear about the suffering among the German people, and it made me doubly grateful for the United States and all the opportunity that it represented.

The Sewing Shops
House of Fine Fabrics

Chapter Four

A Shock—And Growth

Labor Day 1971 was like any other late summer day in Washington—warm and sunny, the skies clear, with just a hint of fall in the mornings and evenings. Ray and I were entertaining friends on our back patio—just a few people gathered to enjoy the holiday and share a meal on a warm summer evening. Everything seemed to be as it should.

But suddenly, in the middle of our meal, Ray started to feel sick and went inside to the bathroom. He looked very gray, so I followed him in, only to find him slumped on the bathroom floor. I stayed with Ray to comfort him,

Model wearing bolts of fabric from a 1970's ad for "The House of Fine Fabrics" in the *Washington Post*.

to take his hand, while Mr. Hank ran to phone the emergency room. Everyone did what he or she could, but it was to no avail. Ray passed away at the hospital later that evening, just as day was turning into night.

It was a heart attack. These days, of course, he might simply have had a bypass—but in 1971 the operation did not exist. Ray's death was a quick one, though not necessarily unforeseen. Heart trouble ran in his family; his niece had passed away in her twenties from heart problems.

Ray's death naturally was a deep shock to me. Ray had been my husband and business partner for more than twenty years. We had spent long hours together, building the business that was our dream, planning and working side by side. Over the years we had become a well-coordinated team, well-matched in our strengths and weaknesses. After so many years, we knew everything about each other. We agreed what had to be done, made our decisions together, and we had reached our goals. Then death intervened, as it often does, unannounced.

During the years we were married, Ray and I had always been in total agreement about what we wanted—we were determined to make a successful life together. I had loved him deeply, and now, still a young woman, I was left alone without my husband. I was devastated but determined to survive and keep our business alive and growing. Needless to say, I feared that I would lose everything we had worked so hard to create. There were, I admit, many nights of fitful sleep when I would wonder if the business would stay afloat.

Of course, any woman would be devastated by the loss of her husband, but it should be remembered that at the time it was hard for a woman to be left suddenly on her own to run a business. It was the early 1970s, and "women's liberation" was just a distant rumbling in America, not something that people had generally come to expect. We have become more accustomed to the fact of successful, public women, but in those days it was almost unknown, a genuine rarity.

I had been younger than Ray, and now I was without him, a widow, another unusual situation for a woman my age in the early 70s. So there I was, a businesswoman in an era that did not think of women in terms of leadership in the worlds of finance, retail, economics, and business. Although we had worked side by side for all those years, Ray once told me, "If anything happens to me, Rose, just sell the business. Sell it for a good price, and retire." After all we had achieved together, he knew that I could run the business by myself. Ray knew me too well to think that I was not able to manage it alone, but he was afraid that others might try to take advantage of me. It is an unfortunate fact of human nature that some people will try to trick a woman in ways they never would a man, simply because they think that a woman could be easily fooled.

Ray's prediction proved correct. Shortly after his funeral, I was approached by several investors who hoped to buy "The House of Fine Fabrics" inexpensively. They thought that in my shaken condition, after the death of my husband, I would neither wish nor be able to run the operations myself, and would have to sell.

But they were wrong. I knew that I could run "The House of Fine Fabrics." By now we had five stores open, and I was confident that I had a sound business plan and a sound strategy for future growth and expansion. I didn't sell the business, even though I was emotionally devastated. I summoned up the determination to keep going—the business that Ray and I had sacrificed so much to build wouldn't simply disappear.

So I carried on, with the help of people like Mr. Hank and my other employees, and continued with our plans for opening new stores, operating fabrics stores that offered our fine products at reasonable prices.

Life went on, and eventually the pain of Ray's death subsided. I am still grateful to Ray for being my partner in those early years, for working so hard when we had so little. I pray for the repose of Ray Benté's soul every day. He was a fine, handsome man, a gentleman—something that too few people are today. His charm and friendliness had helped make the business a success. He was a good manager of people, who knew how to be tough when he had to, but had also earned the respect of everyone who worked for us.

Immediately, I decided to exert a strong hand over the business, closely monitoring the accounts of my rapidly growing company. I always kept close track of the bottom line, remaining aware exactly where every penny of the company's money was spent. Like so many employers, I had to contend with dishonest employees and rampant shoplifting. Theft of all kinds is a significant and discouraging factor in the retail business.

But with Ray's death, I had to take strong action to make it clear that I remained in control of the company, and had to demonstrate that I had the financial and business judgment necessary to keep the organization afloat. Both my employees and the Washington business community had to be made aware that I was not just a wife taking over her hus-

Interior of 2nd store on Connecticut Ave. (near N Street).

band's business, but had, over the past twenty years, developed sound business judgment and managerial expertise of my own. If anyone had any inclinations about taking advantage of a woman boss, he or she soon learned otherwise.

I also had to spend more time visiting each store, at least once a week, especially the ones in the more distant suburbs. I traveled the seventy-mile circular beltway around Washington, visiting as many stores as I could each day, making sure that each store received the attention it needed. In this way, I continued the hands-on approach that Ray and I had used from our modest beginnings in The Sewing Shop on Connecticut Avenue.

There were many people who told me, once I decided not to sell the stores and to continue running them myself, that I would never be able to devote enough time to each store. I think that I proved them wrong. In the years after Ray died, there was not an important decision, a high-level hiring, or a major inventory purchase in which I did not have the final say. Fortunately, those decisions led to another period of rapid growth.

I continued to expand the company, opening more stores around the Washington metropolitan area. I found myself in charge of a growing chain of stores, with larger payrolls, different buying needs, and complex management challenges. I also continued to look for ways to expand our product line. After Ray's death I continued to stay abreast of the new fabrics that were beginning to be popular. The store had already adjusted to the perfection of polyester by the Japanese, the new fabric that became all the rage within months of its introduction to the United States. In these cases, I had to adjust our purchasing quickly once I recognized the changes taking place, but I was able to catch the new fashion wave almost as soon as I saw it coming.

"The House of Fine Fabrics" also moved into the interior-decorating business. Washington was becoming more and more affluent, especially in the suburban areas, and increasing numbers of people wanted personalized help with choosing patterns for couches, drapes, and color schemes inside their homes. This became a very profitable field for us, as our stores could provide both the decorating advice and the fabrics for upholstering and curtains. Soon we were doing a brisk business in interior decoration, with more than thirty decorators on staff in our stores.

As the business grew, I began to be noticed around the nation as one of a new breed of businesswomen who made their fortunes by running their own organizations, making the decisions and plotting strategies—just like the men did. I would be written up in the *Washington Post* and several business publications in New York and California.

The decade of the 70s became the period in which women began to gain acceptance and recognition at the highest levels of business. I am grateful to have been part of that groundswelling generation of successful business women.

But I had lots of help. In those days, I had Mr. Hank, who was the vice president and regional manager, to oversee a group of stores, plus a manager and assistant managers in each store. Most of them were honest people, though I did discover a few dishonest people among the group. Theft—both by customers and employees—is a serious, ongoing problem in the retail industry. If Americans understood how much the price of goods and services is increased by petty theft, they would be outraged.

In my business alone, through the years we lost millions of dollars to theft. In the beginning of the business, there were only a few employees, and Ray and I were right there in the store so frequently that theft was not a problem. But as "The House of Fine Fabrics" began to grow, my managers and I had to take more and more steps to combat theft. First we gave each employee separate cash registers. Earlier there had been one or two cash registers in the store that each salesperson used. But if there is no personal, designated responsibility for the money count at the end of the day, no one can be blamed. Some of our employees took advantage of this, and often there would be twenty dollars missing here, thirty there. So we gave each salesperson a cash register of his or her own. Of course, it was an extra cost to get the new cash registers, but it was necessary to stop dishonesty.

Model draped by a bolt of fabric from "The House of Fine Fabrics" in the *Washington Post*.

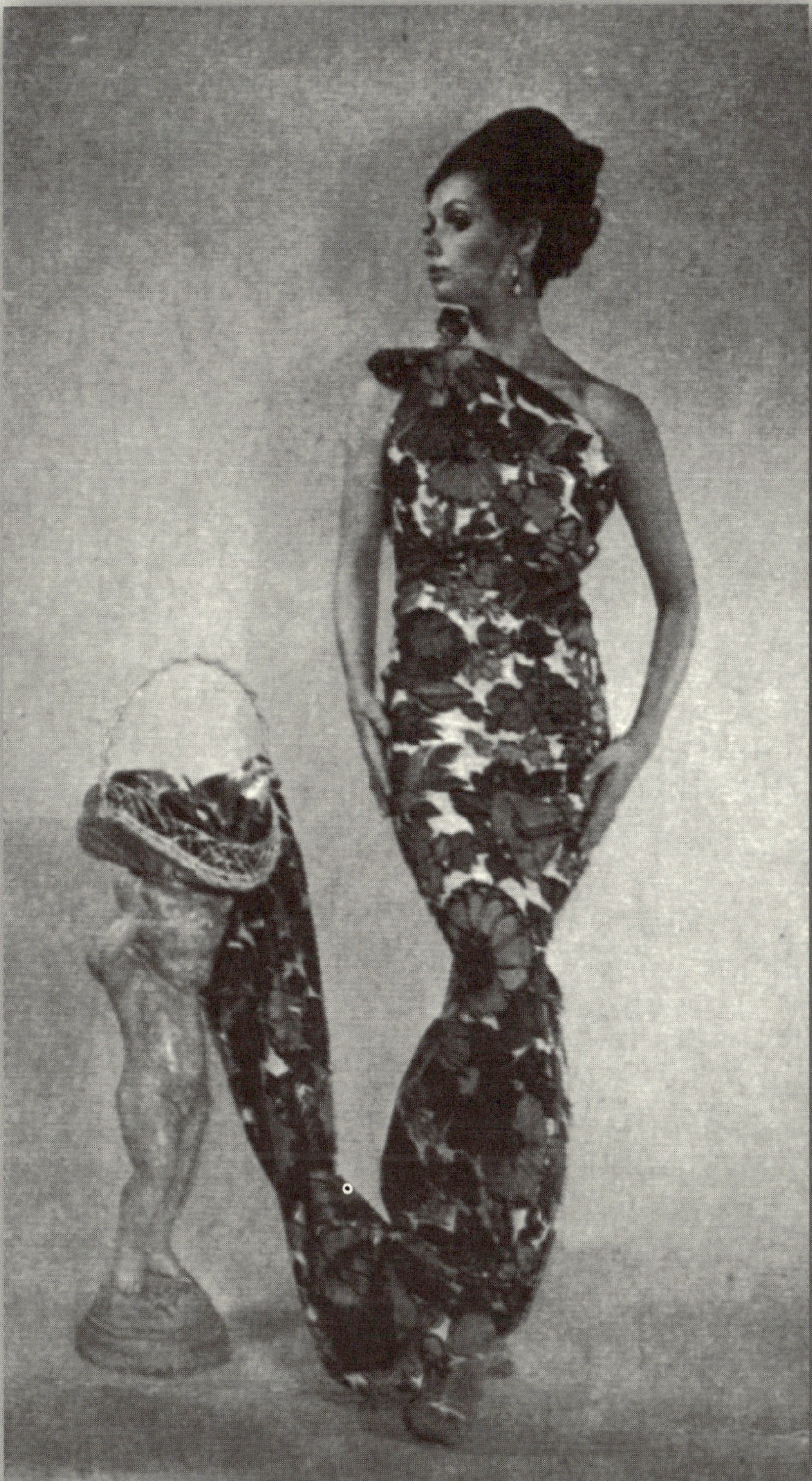

It is this sort of thing—being forced to buy more cash registers because of one employee's theft—that is part of the hidden cost of theft, a cost that is ultimately passed on to consumers in the form of higher prices.

Thankfully, the vast majority of my employees were honest and hard-working and a few of them would stay at "The House of Fine Fabrics" for years, becoming trusted friends—almost like family. Much of the theft came from professional and amateur shoplifters, who would remove buttons, thread, needles, a few extra yards of fabric—anything that they could put in their purse or pants. And sometimes they did not stop there.

In one memorable instance, a group of people came in and distracted all the store's employees. Then an accomplice slipped in, wearing a large coat, and left with one of our portable sewing machines from the display window tucked underneath. This was in the 1970s, when sewing machines were quite a bit bigger, even the portables, than they are today! I have never understood how they got away with it.

Retail, as I'm sure you've noticed from these stories, is a difficult business. It requires that you work very hard and put in long hours; sometimes you suffer setbacks, such as employee theft, that you had not made allowances for at the beginning. By 1978, after years of running the business, both with Ray and by myself, these countless hours began to take their toll on me, and I decided that it was time to sell.

Of course, there had always been offers. In fact, before he died, Ray and I visited the Brown Shoe Co. in St. Louis, Missouri, to hear its offer. The company only wanted to pay for inventory, and at the time we didn't have much in the stores, so we rejected the bid. As I said, once I became a widow I received several offers from people trying to take advantage of my position, but I decided to run the business on my own. But in 1978, seven years after Ray's death, I began to look around to sell the business.

I was contacted by a company in Cleveland, Ohio, called the Fabric Center of America. The company had approached me a few times previously, but, like the Brown Shoe Co. earlier, had only offered to purchase the inventory. I tried to negotiate a sale that included payment for the goodwill of my customers and the reputation that "The House of Fine Fabrics" had built up over the years. But we were just a "rag business," as they called it—its slang term for a fabric store. I remember being rather angry when I heard the company's officials say that about the business I had spent so much time and effort building. I eventually decided to sell the company for all its tangible assets.

When I sold "The House of Fine Fabrics," we had been in business for thirty years and had become an established business in Washington, an important and recognized member of the city's retail community. The store had a solid reputation among customers as the best place to shop for quality products and services, and I had developed a reputation as a tough, shrewd, and honest businesswoman.

I was sorry to see the company sold, though I was happy to be out of retail, away from the hours and the constant struggles to turn a profit. "The House of Fine Fabrics" had succeeded beyond my wildest dreams. When I sold the business, we had a large chain of stores, a warehouse, and almost four hundred employees. In buttons alone, I had more than a million dollars tied up in inventory, to say nothing of fabric, sewing machines, real estate, displays, capital goods, and various other goods.

By anyone's standards, "The House of Fine Fabrics" was an undeniable success. I retained an active interest in the company even after I sold it, serving as a fashion consultant for the business from 1978 until 1983, but I was free of the day-to-day duties of running a growing business. Yes, it was a sad moment for me, but I was also relieved to be done with the responsibilities. I had not stopped working hard from the day I arrived in America from Germany in 1939, so the time, I thought, had finally come to put my efforts elsewhere.

As we were finalizing the sale, I remembered my family's letters to me, written from America when I was a young girl, with their descriptions of how easy it was to achieve financial success in America. As far as I am concerned, those letters were right: You can create success in America, and yes, you can succeed, you can be your own boss and run your own business, if you're willing to sacrifice and save, and work especially hard. "The House of Fine Fabrics" proved to me those promises were true.

Only in America can a young girl come, penniless and without knowing the national language, and build her own chain of stores, making a comfortable life unlike any she might have had back in her own country. I believe this is the best land there ever was, a great land, and a fair land. I thank God every day that I was led to come here to live.

I had sold the company for many reasons: because of the work, the struggles, and the hours. But there was another reason: I had married again, to an extraordinary and distinguished man whose life with me would commence the second part of my life, the story of my American Dream.

Rose showing brocade to designer in 2nd Connecticut Ave. store.

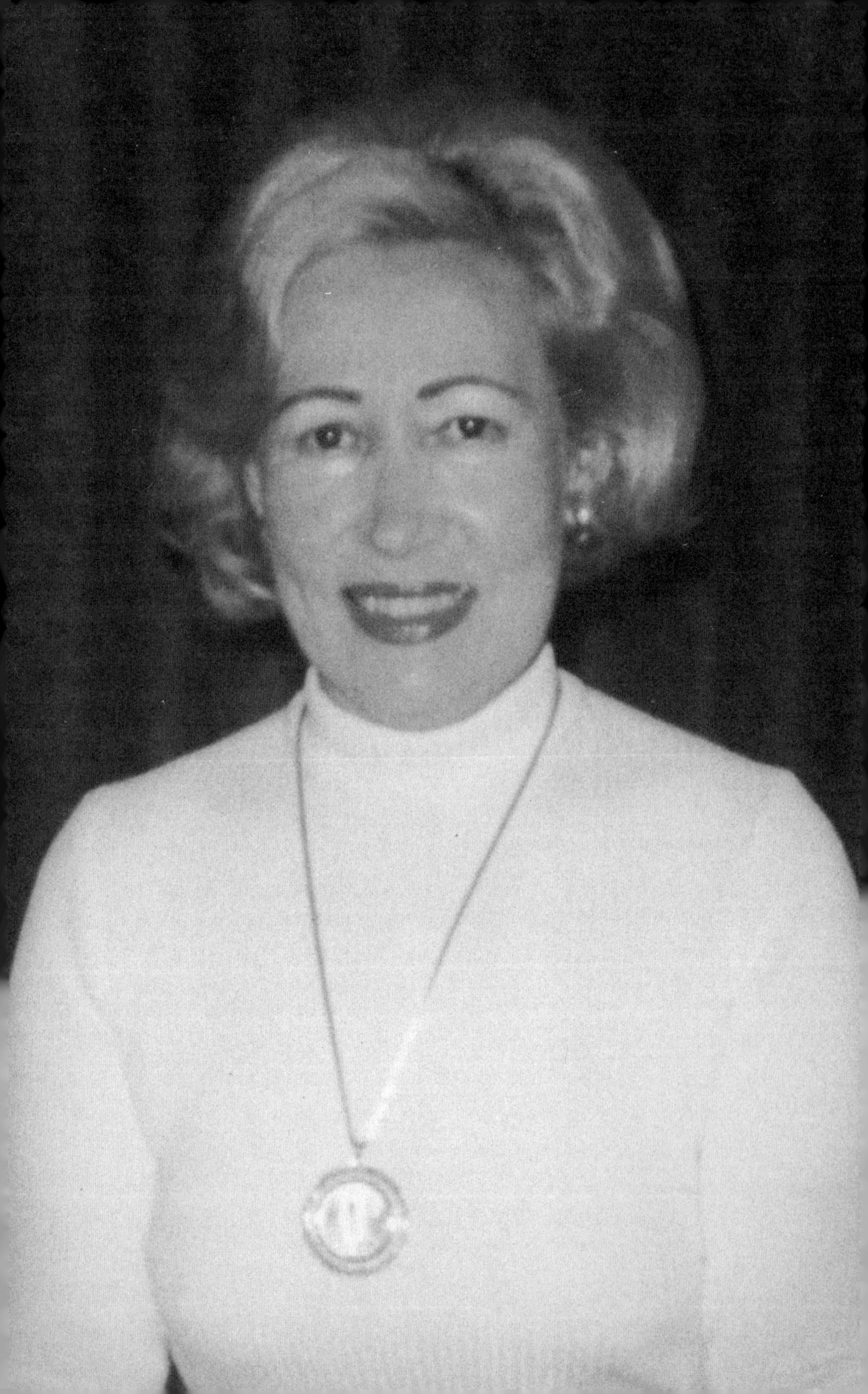

Chapter Five

New Beginning

After Ray died, well-meaning friends tried to set me up. They were sure that I needed the companionship of the local bachelors and widowers. But in those early days of widowhood, I was too busy with the business to really date anyone at all.

My marriage to Ray, and all those years spent building "The House of Fine Fabrics," led me to doubt that I would ever be able to love anyone else. There were times that I would consent to go out with some of these men, but my heart was never really in it. I was, perhaps, a little lonely,

Rose in 1974.

but I was working harder than ever, and there did not seem to be anyone who could fill the hole of that loneliness. When I needed an escort, my trusted Mr. Hank always made himself available.

And then I met Bob Lee. We were at a dinner party arranged by close mutual friends. I liked him immediately—Bob was witty, full of charm and most gracious learning. We spent the entire evening talking, and by the time I left the party we had become well-acquainted. Soon he called me up and we began to date. Bob said that he knew right away that I was the woman he wanted to marry. I told him later that I felt the same way. We did not start seriously dating until he returned from a two-month conference in Geneva, Switzerland.

Our marriage in 1974 was one of the primary reasons in my decision to find someone to buy my business. My way of life began to change drastically: I began to think less about my business and more about my marriage to Bob and our opportunities to travel and visit exotic places like China and Europe. After so many years of constant work, I was being awakened, through my relationship with Bob, to a whole new set of interests. For the first time, my interest in business became secondary.

Robert Emmet Lee was born in Chicago, just before World War I, into an Irish Catholic family. He was not named after the Confederate general, but after a nineteenth-century Dublin rebel who was executed by the

English. The Lees had not been long in America, and the pull of the old country could still be felt as he grew up, a strong influence on Bob from his youth. His father immigrated when he was nineteen and his mother was sixteen—they had known each other in the old country, though they did not marry until they had settled in Chicago. Bob always loved Ireland deeply, and traveled many times to Galway County, the birthplace of his parents, to see the setting of his favorite song, "Galway Bay."

Bob had a colorful early life in the midst of a closely knit family, which gave him more than an Irish "background," but the strong imprint of Irish character, personality, and religion. His smooth delivery in public speaking betrayed the gift of gab so often found on the Emerald Isle, a quality that served him well in the political world of Washington. He was well-known around the country for this kind of wit; his capacity for friendship and lively conversation were valued by all who knew him.

Bob came to Washington and climbed to the top of the Washington pyramid of power. When I first met him, he was the commissioner of the Federal Communications Commission (FCC). His first wife had died in 1972, after a long struggle with cancer, and he was considered one of the most eligible bachelors in town. Bob introduced me to a side of Washington I had long witnessed from a distance but now could see from the inside—its political and social life. Bob was an important policy-maker who knew everybody, and anyone who did not know him wanted to meet him. He is still credited as the architect of modern telecommunications policy. It is indicative of the quality of his mind that he could command respect in a field as complicated and ever-changing as this. His interest and involvement in communications spanned the years of the greatest advancements in communications technology, and Bob was widely praised for his prudence and expertise in guiding this growing field.

Bob's career in Washington began in 1938 as a favorite assistant to J. Edgar Hoover during the formative years of the Federal Bureau of Investigation. A close friend to Senator Joe McCarthy, Bob watched with dismay as McCarthy destroyed himself and many of those around him. Bob became the chief congressional investigator for the House Appropriations Committee in 1946. Fortunately, in 1953 President Eisenhower nominated Bob to serve at the FCC, where he was reappointed by four presidents, serving twenty-eight years—the longest term of any commissioner in FCC history. The length of this record of appointed service to the country is unmatched by anyone in this century.

After his retirement in 1981, Bob remained active in the communications field, serving as a consultant for several companies, even becoming involved in satellite communications technology, and laying the groundwork for the great evolution of satellite-based cable television (the results of which, unfortunately, he never saw). He was also a consultant to Fletcher, Heald and Hildreth, a law firm in the Washington suburb of Rosslyn, Virginia.

Bob had a great love for the Catholic faith—his entire life was lived in close communion with the Church. Religious broadcasting was a special interest of his. He believed that religious broadcasters could responsibly serve God's purpose and the nation's needs. But he was also worried about those who misused their sacred and legal trust for their own financial profit. Bob took the lead in founding the Catholic Apostolate of Mass Media, which has offered sound guidance to Catholic broadcasters and other faith-based media operators. He was very proud of this organization, and his spirit still guides its work.

For his work on behalf of the Catholic Church, Bob was eventually invested as a Knight of Malta (Federal Association)—an honor of which he was most proud until the end of his life. Other Catholic organizations that he was active in included the Thomas More Society and the Brent Society.

Despite all the honors, Bob remained a down-to-earth person. He was quick with a joke or a quip and had a marvelous sense of humor, and he never let himself become a snob or lose touch with his Irish Chicago roots. I remember once, after we had married but before I sold my business, Bob was incensed because he was sure that one of my employees was stealing. So he went in to the Chevy Chase store one Saturday to cut fabric and keep an eye on the offender. While he was there, Barbara Walters, the ABC newscaster, came in to purchase a few items. Imagine her shock at seeing the commissioner of the FCC measuring and cutting beautiful fabric in a shopping center on the weekends! For years, whenever Bob thought about that story, he laughed.

He also moved right in to the little home Ray and I had built in Arlington. I had decided to build a much larger, much fancier home in McLean, a very posh suburb of Washington, but Bob said "no," he would prefer to stay right where we were. Bob was a man who could have been part of the wealthy, upscale elite life, but he preferred a quieter existence. He was not a man who needed a lot of money or awards to make him happy.

Bob once wrote me a poem about the house I built that we never moved into—it is filled with his good humor and keen wit. It provides a real glimpse of the man who was my friend and husband during those years:

"The House That Rose Built"
by Robert E. Lee
(September 1987)

Some years ago in Deutschland
a hübsch mädchen dreamed
of a land of milk and honey
(or was it silk and money?).

It came to pass, the dream came true,
but roses fear uprooting
from soil warmed by ancient time
to steamships that are tooting.

She spoke to all who listened
but they could *nicht verstehen*
this *schön kind* with pigtails
who came from far awayen.

She wept at first, then set her chin
"This wall I'll cut like tin
I'll go to school and show these fools
A REAL AMERICAN."

Her background was in fashion,
but this was hard to sell
She had a German accent
when French was *Haute Modelle*.

But she bought a bolt of fabric
and severed it in two
and put it in *das fenster*
on Connecticut Avenue.

The passersby rushed in to buy
from Rose, whose dedication
commenced an empire soon to be
respected through the nation.

This house of fashion prospered
so as the years went by
it was a golden asset
that many wished to buy

When the time seemed prudent
she sold the whole *geschaft*.
to use the funds for charity
for those who were bereft.

Rose gave to every cause she could
and loved it all intensely
but found to host these worthy groups
her home was all too empty.

"A larger home I surely need,"
she said to many friends
and started off to find a house
that suited means and ends.

Rose looked and looked
without much *glück*
since none met her approval
I'll build my own, decided she
Control my own removal.

To build a house, I needn't say
is really not so simple
In fact, if I could tell the truth,
you're in up to your dimple.

> The architect, the builder,
> electrician, and the plumber
> need all be told in great detail
> by people they deem dumber.
>
> But when the work starts
> taking shape
> and neighbors crowd to ogle
> the German girl in Rose will bloom
> the clever...and the frugal.
>
> I'll bet my poke that when it's done
> Rose sells it for the dollahs
> and builds herself another one
> It's business *über alles!*

In addition to his many accomplishments, Bob's formal education included a law degree from De Paul University in 1935. His amazing career then went on further: He received honorary doctorates from Notre Dame, St. John's University in New York, and St. Bonaventure University. Now from that moment on, the Irish Chicago youth from the South Side was known as "Dr. Lee." Bob was proud to be associated with these fine institutions, especially Notre Dame, where he was asked to offer each year a special week of seminars and lectures on his field of expertise, telecommunications.

Bob died while writing his autobiography. One thousand people attended his funeral Mass at St. Matthew's

Cathedral in Washington; more than twenty priests stood at the altar and James Cardinal Hickey eulogized him.

I did not want Bob's efforts at telling the marvelous story of his life to go unfinished. So I pieced Bob's thoughts together, and with the help of a writer, completed the manuscript, which was accepted for publication by University Press of America in the autumn of 1995. It was entitled *In the Public Interest: The Life of Robert Emmet Lee from the FBI to the FCC.*

On December 5, 1995, at a publication party, a book-signing, attended by more than three hundred of Bob's friends and colleagues, we gathered to celebrate the memory of Bob. We crowded into Mr. Day's, one of several restaurants owned by Bob's son, Bobby. This was a perfect setting—warm, congenial, Irish, and a short walk from the FCC. It was the restaurant at which Bob ate lunch frequently. It was also the site of Bob's "wake."

Fr. Ned Joyce of Notre Dame, who had been President Theodore Hesburgh's right-hand man in Notre Dame's heyday of campus expansion, presided over the lunch and booksigning ceremony. Several former FCC commissioners and the elite of the Washington communications community were there to honor Bob as well. I was grateful for the presence of all these friends and wellwishers, whose presence made a cold and rainy day warm with friendship and love. I said in my remarks at that gathering:

Dear friends—what a great day! Thank you for coming to celebrate this book's release. I know that Bob is with us in spirit, smiling down from his heavenly vantage point.

Bob worked on this book for many years. He wanted to share his life and experience with you—and it was a remarkable life. In these pages, you will read about the beginning of the FBI, Bob's work in Congress, and his almost twenty-eight years at the FCC.

But this is also a book about Bob's love for people. He had a deep, lasting, Irish love of life. And he had an infinite love of the Catholic Church, of Notre Dame, and of Ireland.

This book captures Bob's wisdom, his generosity, and his loving spirit. It is a little part of Bob we can all share. Let me thank John Sisk and the University Press of America for agreeing to publish Bob's work. I know that Bob would have been so proud of this book.

The best way to remember Bob is to enjoy this party and each other's company. And I hope that you will read this remarkable book—Bob's book. Thank you all for coming.

Bob, I am sure, was looking down from heaven and was sorry he missed that party. He would have loved to have been there that day, with his friends and coworkers. He was that sort of man—he loved gathering his friends and family around him to remember old times, to laugh and joke, and to share fellowship with the people he loved.

His love, warmth, and influence are a constant presence in my life and that of his three children, his twenty grandchildren, twelve great-grandchildren, and his friends. He was, no doubt, present at that book party in spirit, I know.

Bob's life, like mine, was a story of rising from humble beginnings to prominence in this land of America, a land he loved as much as I do. Bob would have never accepted the idea that the American Dream is over, that the old ideals that make this a great country are no longer relevant in the twentieth century. He was a true American patriot, and he left behind a legacy of public service unsurpassed in modern Washington.

Bob Lee was a man of great and recognized quality, and the proof of this is the high regard in which he is still held throughout the world. His fine reputation has continued to be talked about long after his passing in 1993, proving that the quality of a person is the real legacy he or she leaves behind. I pray for him every day, and I am confident he looks down from heaven and blesses all of us who honored him that day.

Rose and husband Bob with Msgr. Knott at St. Agnes Church in September, 1974.

Rose Benté Lee

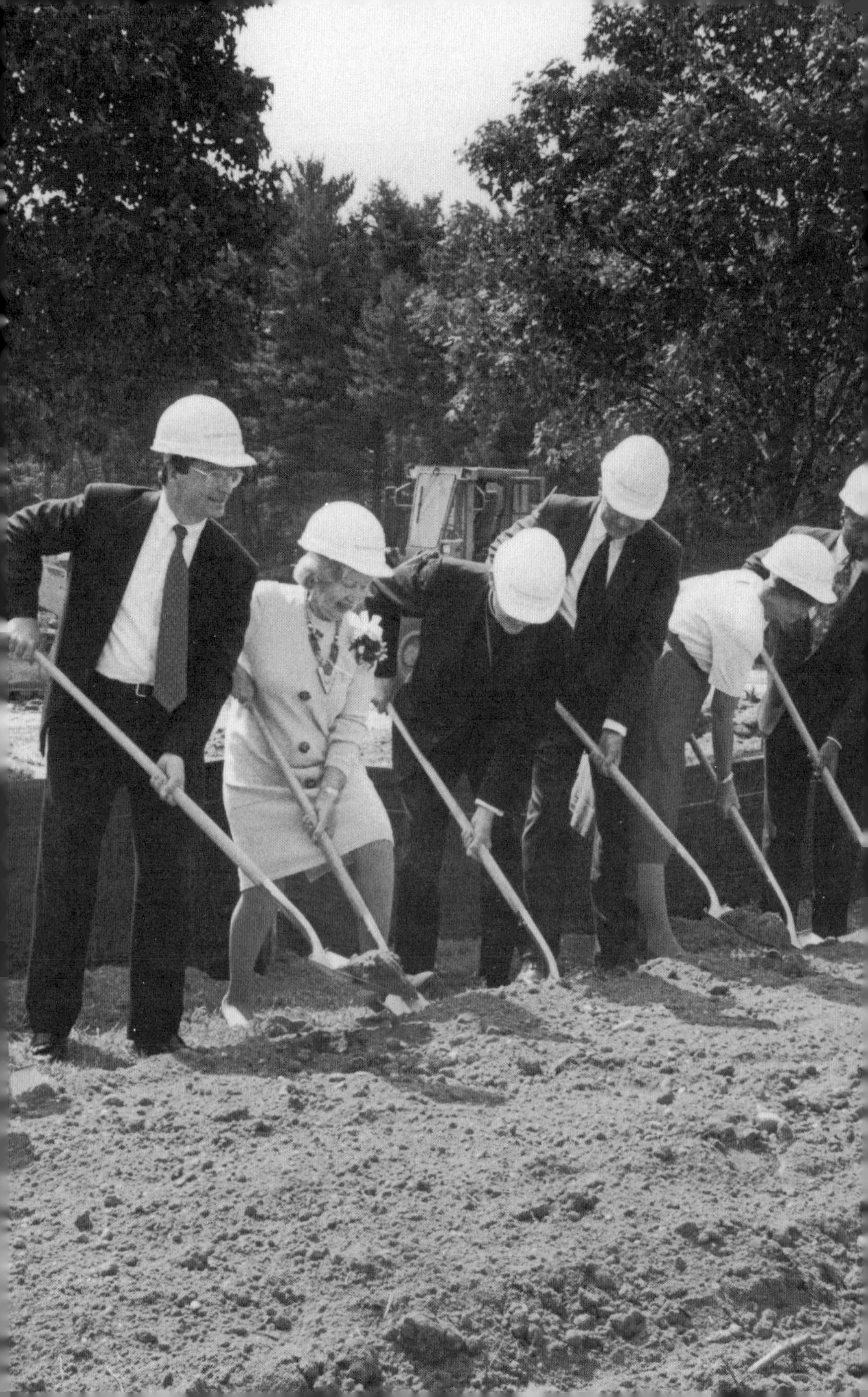

Chapter Six

Gratitude and Giving

On reflection, in considering the humble beginnings of my life, the subsequent uncertainties and sometimes faltering steps as I progressed through my life in accomplishing my goals, I cannot but realize that there was a supportive and guiding hand giving me the inner strength and confidence I would need to reach these goals.

This was my faith in God, in knowing that He would not abandon me in my trials and tribulations, and that he would show me the way through my doubts and periods of despair.

Rose showing Cardinal Hickey how to shovel dirt at groundbreaking for the Malta House, 1994.

This is the faith instilled in me from my earliest childhood by my parents and subsequently through the teachings and guidance of the Catholic Church. It is this faith that inspired me and made possible the final accomplishment of my business ventures and then enabled me to progress to my ultimate and desired life's goal, in accordance with the moral teachings of the Catholic Church: to helping those less fortunate, who were unable to help themselves.

When I was young, in Ruckers-Fulda, everyone around me was Catholic; I went to Catholic schools, my family went to Mass, and we prayed together. Catholicism was everywhere around me, it was what I grew up with, it was my way of life. So, unlike many Americans today who are uncertain about their religion, I have always been blessed with the knowledge that there is a God and that I should pray to Him and obey Him. It never occurred to me that I should do it in any other way. As I look back on it, the Catholic faith was always there in my life, as if it filled my heart through the very air I breathed.

The gift of faith, given to me by family at home, has been the foundation of my entire life, and the key to my ability to succeed through all the struggles I have previously described. Since my retirement, I have resumed going to Mass more frequently, something I was never able to do as a younger woman, because I

Rose and President Ronald Reagan, 1986.

was so engrossed with the mornings at "The House of Fine Fabrics."

In gratitude to the Church, I have attempted to support the Church's works, including corporal works of mercy for the poor, Catholic education, and support for the church I attend in Arlington, Virginia, St. Agnes Parish, where I pray every day for those I have loved and for those who have passed on.

Being a lifelong Catholic helped me to understand that the hunger of the body is only one kind of hunger. There is also the hunger, more importantly, of the spirit and the underlying faith that nurtures the spirit. I decided to do something about the physical and spiritual needs of those around me in the areas of health, children, the arts, education, and the Church, just to name a few.

There is a story from the Bible that inspires me and expresses, perhaps, an example of one of the spiritual reasons why I continue to give what I can to the community around me. In the biblical story of Joseph of Arimathea, Joseph is a prominent member of the Sanhedrin, a man of means, a godly man, and a follower of Christ. After the Crucifixion, Joseph, using his influence before Pontius Pilate, claims the body of Christ and places it in his own personal tomb. It is that tomb, given by Joseph, that is the site of the Resurrection. In his own small way, Joseph of Arimathea contributes to the salvation of the world through his generous gift.

I strongly feel that Joseph of Arimathea's story is a reminder to all successful people: Because you have done well, you have a duty to your community and to your God. And you never know what effect your gift may have—you never know how it may change the world. You will never know, unless like Joseph of Arimathea you walk up to Pilate and take the risk of giving.

Yes, there is a risk in investing in community activities and institutions, just as there is a risk in business. There is the risk that your investment will not reap the benefits you anticipated. Nonprofit corporations, like any for-profit businesses, have to be properly managed, and must have a sound business plan and a clear mission. This is the challenge of philanthropy. I have tried to be discriminating and careful in the resources I have provided. I am proud of my investments in relieving both the hunger of the body and of the spirit—I can happily report that they have prospered.

Just as growing "The House of Fine Fabrics" was my challenge before, now managing my community investments is the challenge I face today. I constantly look for ways to help, like a physician looking beyond the physical symptoms for the root problem that needs treatment. This is how I have tried to help others and the community, supporting causes that will reap benefits over time and well into the future. In the following chapters, I will explain how I have gone about taking the philanthropic risk in the footsteps of Joseph of Arimathea.

I think my attitude toward community giving is best summed up in a speech I gave to the Knights and Dames of Malta at the dedication of the Malta House for the elderly and dependent, given in memory of Robert E. Lee. On that wonderful day, I told those assembled:

Today is an historical moment in the work of the Knights of Malta. We continue the work begun by this organization nearly one thousand years ago, continuing a legacy of caring for the sick and the needy. I am privileged and humbled to be part of this meaningful celebration.

As a child in my native Germany, I watched elderly relatives and family friends

> suffer in their later years, unable to care for themselves. At an early age, I promised God and myself that if I were to prosper in the New World, I would one day try to make a difference in the lives of the elderly poor....
>
> They say that good things are worth waiting for. In this case, Malta House is all we dreamed that it might be—and even more. I am so grateful to God for the opportunity to serve Him and my fellow man by playing a small part in this wonderful moment. My deepest appreciation and thanks to all who have worked so hard for so many years to make this dream a reality.

I think that speech said it best: Service to man is, ultimately, service to God. God, who is the source of everything we have, even our very lives, asks only that we give back to Him through prayer and worship and to others through acts of sacrifice and service. And it is the particular responsibility of those who have been blessed with success to nurture the community that has been so good to them.

Even as a young girl growing up in Germany, I had decided that if I ever had the means I would try to help the elderly and the sick. It was during my marriage to Bob that I realized the time was right to start giving more back

The Malta House.

to the community. I am grateful to have been fortunate in this life, and while most of that good fortune came with hard work and commitment, some of it was made possible with the blessings of God.

As the result of my background and experience, I believed that as a person who had benefited from the support and patronage of others, I should find new ways to invest in the community and the future of the people who live in it.

Before he died in 1993, Bob was very supportive of my efforts—he had a bit of the "lord of the manor" about him and instinctively believed that there was a need for the people with means to share with others. He had witnessed the plight of the Irish immigrant first-hand in Chicago, and he felt deeply about helping people overcome the disappointments of that experience.

In my own life, I was always concerned about the hard times and devastating inflation that Germany underwent between the two world wars. The entire country, as did the world, had suffered from the collapse of the world economy. In part, Germany particularly suffered due to the harsh reparation terms imposed by the League of Nations after the First World War. It was even worse in Germany after the Second World War. The difficulties of my own family during this period were the hardest to watch, which was one of the reasons that I sent for them to work with me in America. Not only would they be trusted and capable workers, but they too could profit from the possibilities of the American Dream.

There were very difficult times in post-World War II Germany, and I remember hearing the stories, once I was able to see for myself, of how Mama and my brothers and sisters were forced to struggle. This image reminds me always of just how important it is to help the disadvantaged, if we are able. That could well have been me in Germany after the war, and my life would have been profoundly different. As concerned as I was, I was grateful for the opportunity to be in the United States and living my dream. It is important that we act on those feelings of gratitude for God's gifts in a way that helps others rebuild their lives.

It is often said that success demands responsibility within the community. The trouble is that too many people smile and nod when they hear this, while continuing to operate on the assumption that a business is only a vehicle for profit, a concern for the bottom line. Business must also provide a means for community improvement. Fiscal success comes with a price, the price of fiscal investment, but we often forget that the people of the community need the same kind of opportunity to thrive. As with a business, the greater the investment, the more the people will thrive, and therefore the more a community will be able to provide for the needs of the local businesses. If the needs of those who are without opportunity or encouragement in life are ignored, everyone will suffer in the long term, including those trying to keep their businesses afloat.

There is an inherent duty for those who have resources to work to improve our community and our nation. As the Bible says, "To whom much is given much is required." A true duty is an imperative that admits no exceptions. Successful people sometimes get the feeling that they are the exception, and they sit on their financial resources, treating them as a miser would. They are exceptions, but not of that kind—their success gives them exceptional responsibilities for sharing the resources that they have been blessed with. These material resources must be put to work to make life better, not just for those who have them but also for those who are in need.

Oftentimes when people get older they complain about being lonely and isolated. With the loss of friends and relatives, people can end up alone with the belongings they have worked so hard to gain. Community involvement gets you out of the house, out of doors among people who need help to accomplish their intended good works. There is no greater source of joy.

Those who have succeeded need not isolate themselves behind closed doors, in opulent houses, country clubs, and extravagant parties. These things are fine to enjoy but not as an end in themselves—that is a sure road to developing a cold heart, cynical mind, and selfish spirit.

Rather, success gives people a special opportunity for growth, the opportunity to get involved and make a real difference in their community. These people bring with them their acquired wisdom, fiscal skills, and monetary resources and can make them all available to needy people in order to make their communities prosperous, healthier, more secure, and more productive.

I now think of my life as being divided into two parts. In the first half, I was a businesswoman, living my American Dream of hard work and success. In the second half, after disposing of my business, "The House of Fine Fabrics," I have attempted to repay my country for the opportunities it has given me to live that dream—and, of course, to give glory to God by attempting to do good on His earth.

Giving back to the community has always been a strong impulse in my family. My brothers and sisters were all prominent people in their respective communities, and many of them, especially Anton, Karl, and Englebert, all prominent builders and businessmen—were honored after their deaths for their spirit of public service.

I, too, from an early age was motivated to give to the community around me, especially to the poor. Even as a young businesswoman, well before I truly could have been called successful, I gave to organizations that worked with the poor, trying to help them meet their worldly needs. I believe it was the example of my parents, my faith in God, and the teachings of the Church that gave me the eyes of compassion and the willingness to share a portion of what I had owned—much as Joseph of Arimathea gave his own burial plot to the crucified Christ.

*Rose and Bob with Barbara Bush at opening of
Childhelp facility in Culpeper, Virginia.*

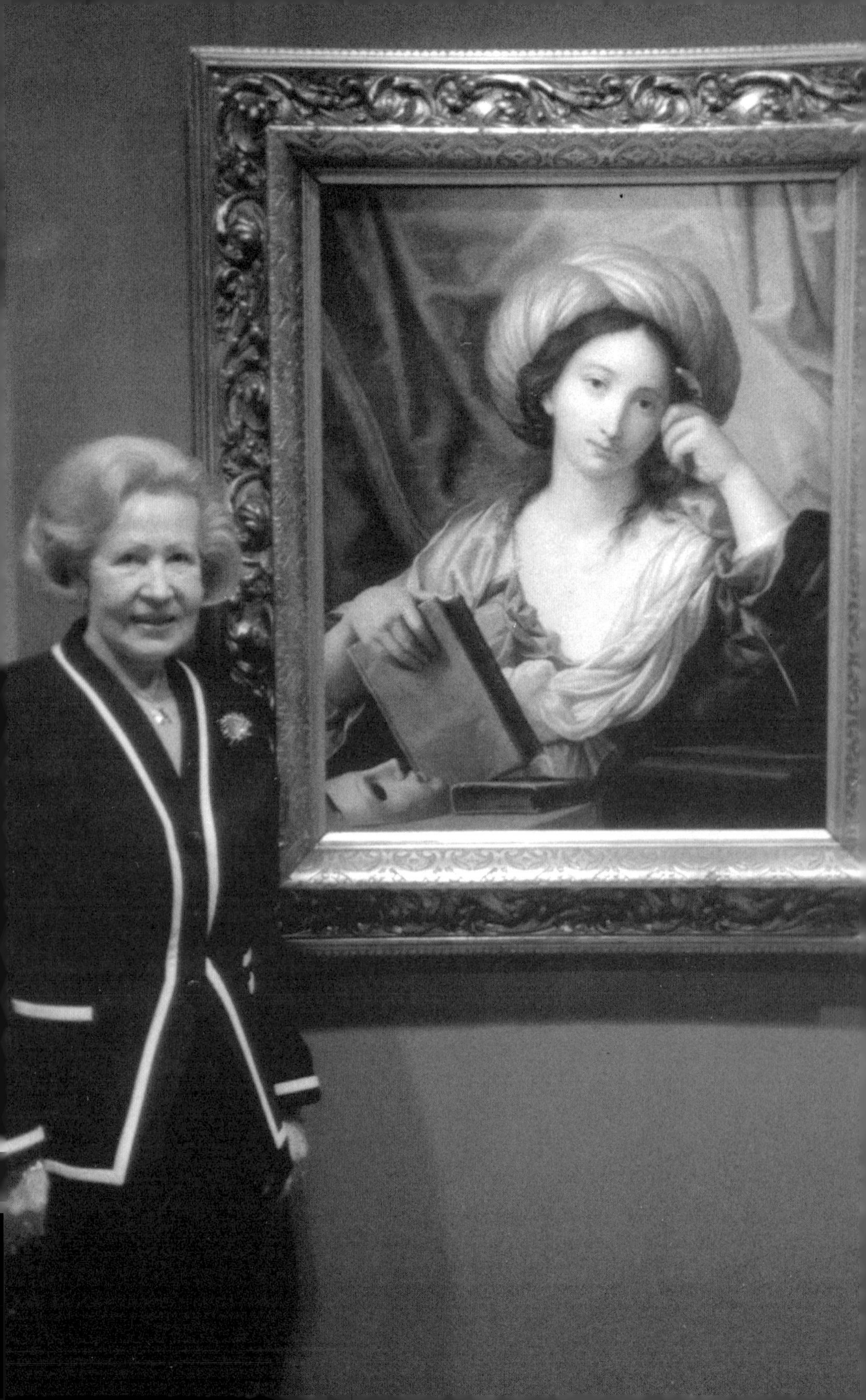

Chapter Seven

Living Through the Arts

I have always loved the arts and believed in their power to lift the human spirit. In the years following the sale of my business, Bob and I spent many evenings attending the opera, the ballet, and the theater. To this day I cannot help but admire the amount of work that artists must do to create the kind of beauty they bring to the stage and communicate to the audience. Excellence, as I had learned myself, always comes at a great price, and our artists are wonderful examples of the beauty that persistence and discipline can create.

Rose at the National Museum of Women in the Arts, Washington, D.C.

As a business women involved in the world of fabrics and fashion, I was acutely aware of the human need for beauty. In my own way, I was an artist concerned with how people adorn themselves through the fabric and design of their clothes. The choice of clothing is perhaps the most obvious way we express our basic need for beauty. As a dress designer, I am attuned to the need for a compelling visual presentation. I am drawn to the visual, my eye looking at the use of color, form, technique, and vision within a medium. In fact, I used to enjoy painting.

There is nothing merely physical about this interest in beauty. Beauty is part of the spiritual hunger so often overlooked in a society preoccupied with material needs. The cultural institutions devoted to the arts are primarily responsible for addressing this spiritual need through maintaining a high level of excellence in the performing arts available to the general public. The death of a symphony, an opera company, a ballet, or a theater is something that we should regret, and something we should be determined to avoid. Television and radio are no substitute for the experience of a live performance of *The Magic Flute*, Beethoven's Ninth Symphony, or a Shakespearean drama.

Unfortunately, the cost of these live productions and exhibitions cannot be met by box-office receipts alone—they must be subsidized by donations or they will disappear from our culture. A culture without live performances and displays of our artistic masterpieces, especially to the new generations of young people, will be a greatly diminished one. When the basic need for beauty goes unfed, history shows that human beings will turn their energies toward vulgar and destructive outlets.

In addition to the performing arts, I have been deeply involved in an important initiative in the plastic arts. In my quest to help meet the spiritual and cultural needs of our citizens, I have been very concerned about the availability of visual art, particularly by women painters, photographers, sculptors, and jewelers.

There are many fine collections of art in Washington: the National Gallery of Art, the Phillips Collection, the Corchoran Gallery, and many private or semiprivate collections. But for me, the best is the National Museum of Women in the Arts (NMWA). Founded in 1981, the NMWA recognizes the "achievements of women artists of all periods and nationalities by exhibiting, preserving, acquiring, and researching art by women and by educating the public concerning their accomplishments." This museum has arguably the finest collection of works by women artists in the world.

Since moving to its present location in 1987, the NMWA has presented more than 120 shows featuring the work of women artists such as Camille Claudel, Margaret Bourke-White, Carrie May Weems, and Dame Elisabeth Frank. It also offers hundreds of educational and outreach programs for children, adults, and teachers. A good example of a broad donor base, the NMWA now boasts 175,000 members supporting the museum and its programs. This makes the NMWA the third largest museum in the world when measured by its membership.

The story behind the creation of the museum begins with the private collection of Wilhelmina Cole and Wallace Holladay, who began collecting art by women in the 1960s. At the time there was a growing awareness of the underrepresentation of women in the art collections of major galleries and museums. The Holladays commited themselves to finding and preserving a body of distinguished work, more than three hundred creations by female artists. Lead by Cole and Holladay, the NMWA was incorporated in December 1981, with the Holladay collection as the foundation of the museum's permanent collection.

The NMWA operated as a "museum without walls" for several years. In 1983, along with many others, I became a founder, donating funds to help purchase a Washington 1907 landmark building, the 70,000-square-foot Masonic Temple located near the White House. Subsequently the building became a masterpiece of architectural achievement, complete with marble staircases, wide rooms, high ceilings, and a dramatic use of construction space. It took more than four years to refurbish and was opened in 1987 to house the permanent collection and inaugural exhibition, "American Women Artists, 1830-1930."

Rose in the foyer of the National Museum of Women in the Arts.

Rose Benté Lee

As a woman who broke ground in the world of commerce and business, I can appreciate the need for a special place where the contribution of women painters and sculptors can be displayed. No one argues with the fact that the great works of woman artists have been overlooked and underappreciated. Both my support for NMWA and my seat on its National Advisory Board are especially satisfying for me because I am helping other woman break through to receive the recognition that they deserve. It took this kind of investment to bring the work of artists like Fontaine or a great sculptress like Camille Claudel, whose "The Gossips" and "Young Girl with a Sheaf" are displayed, to the attention of the general public. Claudel's struggle for recognition in the Paris of the 30s led her toward a total physical and mental breakdown.

The museum is still young and growing. Recently I helped establish the sculpture gallery in the new wing of the museum. The work of the sculptresses Louise Newelson and Frida Baranek are already on display in this room, beautifully lit by an enormous window. This dynamic museum has already led to a greater appreciation of women in the arts and encouragement for women who might have never stayed in the arts. I hope that my support of the NMWA, along with the support of so many others, will make the way easier for those women with the talent and determination to succeed. This remark by Louise Otto-Peters, in 1849, displayed on the wall of the exhibition, sums up my attitude: "The history of all times, and of today especially, teaches that...women will be forgotten if they forget to think about themselves."

I was also privileged, as a "Friend of the First Ladies," to support the exhibition, "The First Ladies: Political Role and Public Image," which opened in early 1992 at the National Museum of American History and closed in 1996. The gowns of the first ladies had been part of the Smithsonian collection since 1914 but had suffered extensive damage from extended display. As chance would have it, the Museum of American History actually repaired the dresses at a shop near my Suitland store. Given my experience in repairing damaged fabric and dress design, I was delighted to consult on this project. When I was shown the distressed condition of Mary Todd Lincoln's dress, I was doubtful it could be fully repaired, but it looked wonderful in the exhibition.

Instead of exposing the gowns to more damage, which would have had to be repaired, this exhibition developed a broader approach, not dependent on the individual gowns but including many artifacts from the First Ladies Collection not previously exhibited, from White House programs and invitations to popular culture materials and political campaign items.

Twenty-eight items of clothing were displayed with other gowns being rotated in and out of the exhibition. Gowns of first ladies exhibited included those of Dolley

110 *An American Dream*

Madison, Lucy Hayes, Julia Grant, Frances Cleveland, Lucretia Garfield, Eleanor Roosevelt, and Jacqueline Kennedy, as well as yellow leather embroidered shoes attributed to Abigail Adams, a gold bracelet watch of Mary Todd Lincoln, and a hand-painted, porcelain hand mirror belonging to Grace Coolidge.

Once again I was helping put the spotlight on powerful and influential women whose contribution to American life had been overlooked. Given my experience with Ray in starting "The House of Fine Fabrics," I found that I could relate easily to women who had been strong personalities behind the scenes, and then, when circumstances made it necessary, had to walk directly into the spotlight. The mission of the exhibit, one of the most popular in the history of the Smithsonian, was "to present the first ladies not as icons, nor as women who married men who eventually became presidents—but as historical agents in their own right."

They adapted their established roles as mothers and wives in political life. The first ladies were great advocates for charities and social change. They were the nurturers of their families and communities. In this way, the first ladies were models of female leadership, even during times when women did not hold political office. The first ladies were the strength behind their husbands' presidencies.

As a Friend of the First Ladies project, I was privileged to join in support of this program with all the living first

Rose with Camille Claudel's "Young Girl With a Sheaf."

ladies, including Barbara Bush and Nancy Reagan. As with the case of the NMWA, the "First Ladies" exhibition had been given an opportunity to support a cause that would draw upon the skills of fabric, costume, and design developed over my entire career.

In Washington, there is another institution that has stood as a beacon of artistic hope and spiritual health—The John F. Kennedy Center for the Performing Arts. The Kennedy Center is home to the National Symphony Orchestra, the Washington Opera, the Washington Ballet, and many fine "road" productions of theater and musical comedy. I am proud to have been a financial supporter from its beginning in 1974. This monument to the importance of the performing arts in our nation stands on the site of an old brewery, commanding a stunning view of the Potomac, and is one of our capital's most popular attractions.

During the day, tourists swarm into the Hall of Nations, admiring the enormous bust of John F. Kennedy or the various foreign flags that signify the international need for arts in the world community. The ticket office caters to the daily performances in the Concert Hall, the Opera House, the Eisenhower Theater, and the Terrace Theater. The Kennedy Center is the epicenter of culture in the nation's capital, rippling out to influence artists and audiences across the United States and as far away as London, Paris, Sydney, and Rio de Janeiro.

But the Kennedy Center is more than a beautiful building with a newly renovated Concert Hall. It is a beehive of supporters, volunteers, employees, managers, and directors. Its board members are chosen from across the nation, representing the worlds of politics, business, and the media as well as the arts. The Kennedy Center is a vast cooperative endeavor, bolstered by the financial support of Congress, a large number of corporations, and many individual supporters from around the world.

Harold Evans, my accountant for many years, suggested that I support the Kennedy Center, and I thought immediately of underwriting some box seats in the Opera House. The incentive was irresistable—I wanted to be a part of creating a first-rate facility for opera in the most important political city in the world. I agreed, and the investment has been satisfying in every way. The Opera House itself is superb, and the box seats, as anyone who has had the pleasure of sitting in them knows, are worthy of such a magnificent facility.

The Opera Company, after overcoming some tremendous financial challenges, is now moving in the right direction under the care of the great tenor, Music Director Placido Domingo, and a hard-working board of directors. We now stand on the verge of developing a world-class opera company. Studies have repeatedly shown that opera has a growing and sustained appeal to younger audiences and an escalating interest with older age groups. With its great spectacle and enveloping drama, opera is an art form for everybody, and almost everybody who gives it a try seems to love it. The Italians have always known this about opera, and we in the United States are just beginning to discover it.

In earlier generations, support for the performing arts came from the well-heeled, old-money classes, or the new rich who wanted to buy respectability. Opera, classical music, and the ballet were supported by the rich for their own benefit. But since midcentury in this country, these performing arts have become more known and loved by all classes of people, regardless of their economic or social status. For the last four decades, there has been a greater accessibility of all the arts for everyone, and the Kennedy Center has been at the forefront of that movement. At a typical performance, you can see the Virginia landed gentry rub shoulders with newly arrived immigrants from South America, and congressmen sitting next to college students.

One reason for this change in audience is that the places where opera, classical music, and ballet are peformed have become the new public squares of our cities. Places like the Kennedy Center and Lincoln Center in New York City have become gathering spots where people meet, make new friends, and feel once again that they belong to a community. Complexes for the performing arts form a common meeting ground for people of all races and classes—their common interest and bond the uplifting power of great art performed at the highest level.

Of course, for those who attend the concert performances, the experience is unforgettable. In addition to the performances by our National Symphony Orchestra, the Washington Opera, or the Washington Ballet, the Kennedy Center hosts outstanding performers from around the world. Jazz has found a home there, with the Billy Taylor Trio often playing with greats like Nancy Wilson, Ray Hargrove, and Wynton Marsalis. The Washington Performing Arts Society brings in outstanding classical performers, like violinist Ann-Sophie Mutter, pianist Misha Dichter, singer Kathleen Battle, or cellist and NSO conductor emeritus "Slava" Rostropovich. The greatest symphonies of the world play there under the WPAS's sponsorship, including the Boston Symphony, the St. Louis Symphony, the Philadelphia Orchestra, and the Los Angeles Philharmonic. In opera, we have been treated to the San Francisco Opera, the La Scala Opera, and the New York City Opera.

I must confess, however, that I have a special love for the ballet. The years I spent on a special women's advisory committee to the Washington Ballet to help in fundraising were very enjoyable for me. The world's greatest ballet troupes, like the Dance Theater of Harlem, the Paris Opera Ballet, the Twyla Tharp Dance Company, the Kirov Ballet, and the Royal Danish Ballet are frequent visitors to the Kennedy Center. I marvel at the combination of gorgeous costumes, beautiful music, and sheer physical skill of the dancers, each looking so effortless, that makes up the experience of great ballet. The past few years some ballet has moved away from the classics that I prefer, especially the Russians like *Swan Lake* and *Sleeping Beauty* of Tchaikovsky, but I continue to go and support it nonetheless. My fondest memory of ballet is seeing the late Rudolph Nureyev dance in *Swan Lake*—his perfect carriage, his great leaps, and his unforgettable capacity to command attention define perfectly the magnetic appeal of ballet to me.

The importance of a great performance, however, is not confined to the immediate listening audience. These cultural events start a ripple effect that educates and informs the community. For years, political scientists and sociologists have stressed the mediating influences of cultural institutions in the society—those groups that help in forming the values that direct our lives. Churches, schools, nonprofit groups, and other organizations help to transmit a positive set of core values and beliefs to the community, values such as mutual respect, tolerance, hard work, and other beneficial attitudes and actions that make our communities safer, saner, and more secure.

Music, dance, and theater bring people together by providing a shared experience of joy and understanding. They motivate us, keep us young, and teach us about the

Rose with Kennedy Center Chairman of the Board, Jim Johnson.

human condition. We learn to look inward and outward, learning more about ourselves while gaining greater sympathy for one another. In the performances of masterworks, we come to a greater acceptance of our faults and failures, as well as tempering our success and good fortune. From *Othello* we learn about the destructive roots of jealously. In Mozart's *Magic Flute,* we recognize the necessity of forgiveness to overcome the legacy of hatred. Who can see the ballet, *Firebird* and not be moved at its climactic finale? Who could hear the music of Duke Ellington and not be brought to a smile? Who is unable to feel the possibilities of human brotherhood in the last symphony of Beethoven? And who is blind to the common experiences of love and pain in *Carmen*? In the words of the great art critic Bernard Berenson, these experiences are "life-enhancing" because they reveal the deepest needs and aspirations of our common humanity. As the late cellist Pablo Casals said of his devotion to a daily playing of Bach on the piano:

> *I cannot think of doing otherwise. It is a sort of benediction on the house. But that is not its only meaning for me. It is a rediscovery of the world of which I have the joy of being a part. It fills me with awareness of the wonder of life, with a feeling of the incredible marvel of being a human being.*

Given the power of art to touch our lives, we must make the arts available to as many people as possible. For this reason, I fully support two recent actions by Music Director Leonard Slatkin and the NSO to bring music to the wider community. Slatkin recently arranged for nightly pre-concert music to be provided free at the Kennedy Center as an educational service and as an enticement to build a broader audience. Because there is no charge, price is not a barrier. There has been a growing interest in these concerts that I hope will continue to increase.

The other action has been to expand the number of free concerts given by the NSO around Washington, often in economically depressed areas. In bringing its music, the NSO is bringing hope to the poor, homeless, and infirm. It is also taking classical music into bastions of rap and jazz, winning a new generation of listeners to classical composers. I should add that the NSO has become a challenging orchestra for those who value the status quo, because it often premieres new music that has jazz influences, modern themes, or political meaning. Leadership such as this will keep the NSO relevant to the community and challenging to its core audience. At a recent dinner party, I heard one well-known educator exclaim, "Well, I have to go to the Kennedy Center tonight to get another dose of education from Slatkin." I could not agree more; we never are too old or too sophisticated to learn.

But even more, we must recognize that the arts are a source of inspiration, solace, contentment, and happiness for millions of our citizens. We may work hard, suffer disappointments in friendships, and struggle with our finances or physical health, but the arts can set our minds above this grind of daily toil. They can bestow upon us the graces of joy and comfort. And in these moments, the arts can remind us that life is always worth living, even when the obstacles to earthly success seem overwhelming. Our symphonies, ballets, operas, plays, paintings, and sculptures rank among the greatest of human achievements, and with proper care can continue giving to their audience for centuries to come.

Rose and Bill Ostapenko shortly after their marriage at National Museum of Women in the Arts.

Rose Benté Lee   121

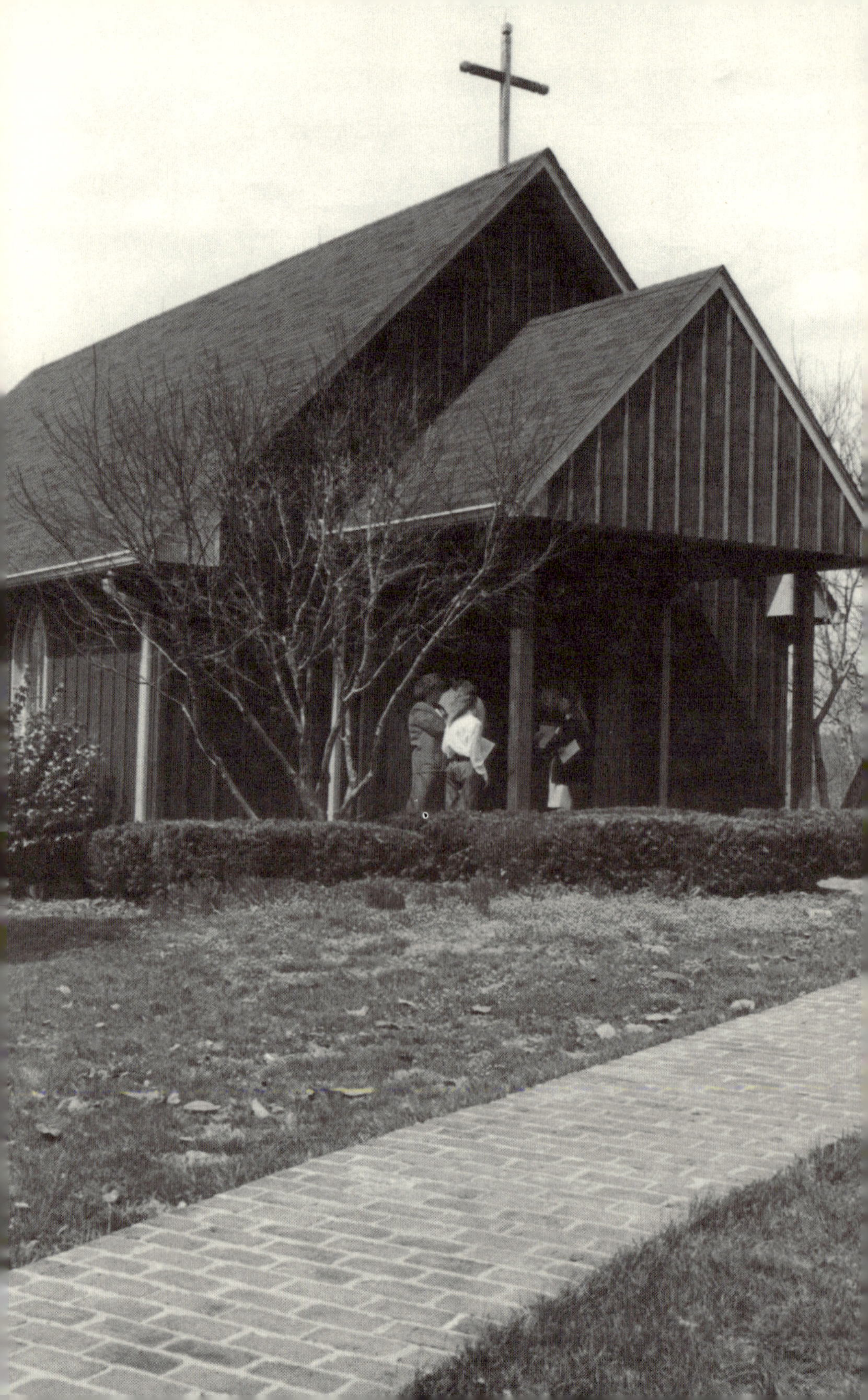

Chapter Eight

A Healthy Community & Children

One of my earliest memories is a desire to help the poor, sick, and elderly. Of course, the deaths of Ray in 1971 and Bob years later only intensified my purpose in doing whatever I could to help institutions who minister to the elderly. Then in 1987, as a member of the Knights of Malta, I became aware of their saying, "Our Lords the poor and the sick," which became for me a good way of summing up my commitment to this cause.

Rose Benté Lee Chapel at Childhelp facility in Culpeper, Virginia.

We do not have to look very far for the principle behind this idea of giving priority to those with physical needs—Jesus said very simply, "love thy neighbor." He did not say this to burden us. On the contrary, one of the greatest of his followers, Mother Teresa of Calcutta, speaks of the joy of faithfully following Jesus's commandment. I have found that whatever I have given to others has been returned to me in ways I cannot even recount.

As I said in the last chapter, it is easily to forget that the needs of the mind for works of imagination to nurture it. This chapter is easier to write: there are few, if any at all, who would deny the need to improve the physical and mental well-being of people everywhere. Government has its role, but it cannot, and should not, be expected to provide everything. Government efforts to provide welfare assistance for those in need through programs like Medicaid and Medicare are absolutely necessary. But millions of people still "fall through" these safety nets. More creative initiatives in the private sector are vital for the well-being of our children, for older Americans, those with special disabilities, and those who require treatment for expensive illnesses.

When Bob contracted cancer, he received treatment at Arlington Hospital in Arlington, Virginia. I was grateful for the quality of care Bob received during his fatal encounter with cancer. He was not treated as another anonymous patient—the hospital staff gave him love, compassion, and the kind of service people need when they are going through traumatic circumstances. They were sensitive to his mental and emotional needs and to his family; they helped to ease our fear, as well as tending to the illness of his body.

I had been involved as a trustee of the hospital since 1971 after Ray's death. I had served from 1979-1988, and Bob had served four of those years with me. Together we had participated in the Hospital's Galen Society, named after the most famous physician of the ancient world and dedicated to helping the poor, and we were its first lifetime members. But when Bob died in 1993, I wanted to do something special for the hospital in Bob's memory. Eventually I donated funds for a new, expanded oncology wing, a special treatment center for cancer patients. A separate oncology unit was needed to meet the special needs of those with cancer. As many people know through firsthand experience, cancer patients often travel a hard and painful road of slow deterioration. Those who make this journey deserve the attention of those specially trained to help them.

The hospital named it the "Robert E. Lee Oncology Unit." Now, with each new patient, this oncology wing offers "state-of-the art" services. Since a likeness of Bob's face graces an entrance to the unit, all these services are delivered with the Irishman's contagious smile. The oncology unit at Arlington Hospital, its programs and staff, is a suitable blessing to his memory.

One of the nicest things about the Robert E. Lee Oncology Unit is the primary nursing approach. This means that when a patient comes into the unit, one of the nurses stays with the patient through his entire hospitalization. The patient becomes the individual nurse's main focus. This creates an unusually close relationship between nurse and patient. Cancer patients often have to be readmitted to the clinic, and very often the same nurse cares for the same patient.

Even though the staff of The Robert E. Lee Unit is about 25 in all, including about 20 nurses, with 19 beds, they are a close-knit group. They purposely take interdisciplinary approach to their patients, with families, doctors, and nurses all working together, often on a first name basis.

I am delighted that the rooms are decorated in comfortable shades of blue and pink. The unit even has a family kitchen, which is soothing to patients because they can bring food from home. Because people have some of their most important conversations in the kitchen, patients are able to chat and relax in a room other than the one that has their hospital bed.

This same kind of integrated, personal care for cancer patients is provided to another hospital program I have supported—the Vincent Lombardi Cancer Research

Robert Edward Lee, Rose, Patricia Lee Fischer, and Michael Lee at the Robert E. Lee Oncology Clinic at Arlington Hospital.

Center at Georgetown University Hospital. The caregivers at Lombardi understand the depth of personal trauma caused by the onslaught of cancer; they "desire to help patients heal physically and emotionally, as individuals and as members of families." However, unlike the oncology center named after Bob, The Lombardi Center is a comprehensive cancer center that not only takes care of patients but also conducts important laboratory research into the prevention and cure of cancer.

In working with the Arlington Hospital, I came to realize that health care is more than the equipment and buildings we see. The health care system is primarily the people we meet, because these are the persons who must care for others in the most difficult of circumstances. Receptionists, physician assistants, physicians, specialists and nurses, all make up the health care team whose job it is to care for the patient as a whole person, not just an individual with a disease. We forget how emotionally challenging it can be to confront day-after-day patients who are dying and families who are around them. Health care professionals must be mature enough to handle the suffering they face—they must intuitively know how to speak and act at the most fragile moments. At their best, these professionals become part of the redemptive experience that suffering, even the physical suffering that prefaces death, can bestow.

The biggest drawback in the healthcare profession at the present moment is the severe shortage of nurses. I became aware of this problem in the 1980s, as a trustee of Arlington Hospital. Without nurses, patients are deprived of information, comfort, hope, and medical expertise. Since they come to your bedside throughout the day, they are in a unique position to make a difference in the lives of their patients. And there was not, and still is not, enough of them.

So, I decided to help increase the supply of qualified nurses by funding a nursing scholarship program at the nearby Marymount University in Arlington, Virginia, where I was also a trustee. Marymount, a Catholic institution in the Diocese of Arlington, already had established a fine reputation for its nursing program. The president at the time, Sister Majella Berg, RSHM, was already familiar to me since she used to come into our store on Connecticut Avenue. She made her own clothes, and I was pleased to give her a special discount. We became good friends and I trusted her—I knew that this scholarship would be administered wisely and fairly under her direction. In 1984 Marymount University established the "Rose Benté Lee Endowed Scholarship Fund," designating scholarships for "needy and qualified students in the School of Nursing." From 1984-1997, 49 students have benefited from the endowment, with 42 having graduated and entered the nursing field, the rest still working towards completion of their studies.

Each year I meet with the current Lee Scholarship students. I am consistently impressed at the commitment and compassion that goes along with their medical training. Marymount University is producing nurses who really love their work and whose care for patients will be improved by the level of their caring. These will be the kind of professionals who cared for Bob before he died. I am honored to be associated with these fine students but even more happy to help add more compassionate and expert nurses into the health care system.

In addition to addressing the shortage of nurses, there are many other health care needs that require immediate attention. As our population ages, with 30 million people over 65 now and that figure likely to double by the year 2030, we need to look after the welfare of our older citizens. Many Americans are simply living longer: the fastest growing segment of our population are those 85 and older. But changing demographics are another reason, as our society becomes top-heavy with older Americans, and younger Americans comprise a decreasing percentage of our population.

I have watched many of my friends lose their ability to care for themselves. Many have moved into retirement homes, assisted living situations, nursing homes, or even hospital settings to receive twenty-four hour care. There is a need for a wide range of choices to meet diverse needs. But any way you slice it, there are not enough good facilities for people to choose from. In Chapter 10, I will discuss the Malta House that I donated to address this problem. Prior to the building of Malta House, I supported the important work of the Hospice of Northern Virginia. HNV is the Mid-Atlantic region's oldest and largest hospice organization. It provides a number of services from its acute care unit to bereavement services to patients and their families—over 5,000 Virginians were served by HNV last year. Many women volunteers are committed to staffing its shelters day and night. Of particular importance in the Patient Care Fund that provides end-of-life services to the indigent, uninsured, and underinsured terminally ill by enabling them to remain at home. And Camp Begin-Again provides recently bereaved children with peer and adult support in a camp environment with activities designed to assist children in coping with their loss. Hospice care services need our support because they treat those who are dying with human dignity by bring comfort, pain control, and a sense of community.

My Catholic faith teaches that we should protect those who are most vulnerable to harm, those who are young and those who are old. Children have also always held a special place in my heart. I did not have any children, but I am very fortunate to be close to my sibling's children

Mrs. Marion Barry (center) and Rose judge the best handmade dolls for the Salvation Army.

and grandchildren, and they are fortunate to have grown up with loving and caring parents.

Many children are less fortunate, coming from broken homes, poverty, poor upbringing, abusive situations, or simply a lack of love and attention. As a young girl I could not have had more loving parents or a greater certainty that they were always on my side praying for me and loving me. Perhaps this is why I have felt a particular calling to help children who are victims of child abuse and neglect. Thus I helped establish Childhelp USA, the largest non-profit organization for the treatment, research, and prevention of child abuse in the U.S., on the east coast. I contributed to the acquisition and maintenance of the Alice C. Tyler Village of Childhelp EAST, a multiservice treatment program situated on 260 acres in Culpeper County, Virginia. The sixty acres in Orange County, Virginia that I donated was sold to help upgrade the beautiful site in Culpeper.

The site of the village itself is far off the beaten track. The children who are accepted there are between the ages of two and twelve with a history of school problems, or, at the risk of abuse or neglect. In the village, children can overcome their behavioral or emotional challenges and can physically and emotionally heal. When the state of Virginia recommends a child be admitted to the Tyler Village, the children come here to receive a variety of services. There is an elementary school for children in grades

Sr. Eymard Gallagher, RHSM, of Marymount University and Rose.

K-7. There are also individual treatment services, in-home services, and a summer camp. The village offers a structured, nurturing environment that assures children feel safe.

The children who come here receive educational services and treatment. The challenges faced by the staff of Childhelp are huge — the state court sometimes sends its "incorrigibles" to be rehabilitated. Parenting classes and family therapy are also offered to the parents and family members of children who live in the village. Childhelp provides funding for the children and often covers expenses for parental travel.

Since I have always understood my philanthropy in the light of my faith, I wanted to provide something that would be of special value to these children — I donated a chapel for private prayer and religious services. The teachers and counselors need to find the spiritual solace that enables them to face the daily challenges of dealing with troubled children. In the midst of the beautiful and remote Culpeper setting I believe that they have a deeply moving physical setting, the chapel helps them to remember that we all can walk with God, and it is to Him we should look when everything else seems to have let us down.

The founding of Childhelp is a wonderful story that demonstrates what can happen when creative and committed people respond vigorously to human need. It started in 1959, when Sara Buckner O'Meara and Yvonne Lime Fedderson were selected out of 500 applicants to represent America on a good-will tour of the Far East. While in Tokyo, Sara and Yvonne "adopted" 11 half-American, half-Japanese homeless orphans they found wandering the streets following a devastating typhoon. They found a home for the children with Mrs. Kin Horiuchi, who lived in a ramshackle, unheated, one-room hut where she was already caring for a group of Japanese/American orphans. The two women promised that money and clothing would be sent to support the orphans, and before they returned home, the number had grown to over 100 mixed-blood children.

Back in the United Sates, Sara and Yvonne began raising funds for their "adopted orphans." Soon the effort began to grow by word of mouth; a nucleus formed and International Orphans Inc. was born and officially incorporated as nonprofit organization in April 1960.

In 1966, Sara and Yvonne were invited to Washington, D.C., and were requested to work with the Third Marine Amphibious Force to help orphans who were victims of the Vietnam War. Five orphanages, a hospital and a school were built and maintained in Vietnam over the next few years. When the American troops left Vietnam, I.O.I. organized the baby lift, bringing thousands of children to the United States for adoption.

As work in Vietnam ended, the grave problem of child abuse was brought to Sara and Yvonne's attention. The Senate Subcommittee on Children and Youth revealed that child abuse in this country had assumed epidemic proportions and the American Medical Association indicated that it was one of the leading causes of death in young children. This caused Sara and Yvonne to redirect the organization's energies and talents toward meeting the needs of abused and neglected children in the United States.

In 1974, under the guidance of the I.O.I. Board of Directors and with the encouragement of numerous childcare experts in both the private and public sectors, they began planning a unique program which would serve as a model treatment plan for abused and neglected children and their troubled families. It was named Children's Village, USA (CVUSA), a project of I.O.I. which would in 1983 be renamed Childhelp USA/INTERNATIONAL. The first residential treatment center, established solely for the victims of child abuse and neglect, opened its doors in 1978. It is located on 121 acres in Beaumont, California.

The organization launched a National Campaign for the Prevention of Child Abuse and Neglect in January 1982 and put into operation the first nationwide toll-free child abuse hotline. A staff of 20 paid professionals and 15 highly trained volunteers manned the hotline which received approximately 60,000 calls annually. This phenomenal growth was helped greatly by first lady Barbara Bush and the Hollywood stars who lent their names and their time to raising funds — Efrem Zimbalist, Jr., Cheryl Ladd, Norm Crosby, Carol Lawrence, Mike Connors, Florence Henderson, Jack Scalia, and the Lennon Sisters have helped raise the millions of dollars necessary to running its programs.

Thanks to these and many others, Childhelp USA is currently the largest nonprofit organization for the treatment, research, and prevention of child abuse in the United States. I am proud to have helped Childhelp fulfill its potential and become a program helping children nationwide.

There are several other well-known national associations that I am proud to have been associated with. As a life member of the Salvation Army Advisory Board, I have met with other community leaders to work with the Corps Officers and advised them on how to raise funds for the Army. Salvation Army is an international movement, an evangelical part of the universal Christian Church. Its message is based on the Bible—"to preach the

Bob and Rose in California with the children of Childhelp USA.

gospel of Jesus Christ and to meet human needs in His name without discrimination."

Although not an explicitly religious organization, CARE USA, a member of CARE International, is a charity I admire greatly and have long supported. CARE is a confederation of 10 agencies that deliver relief assistance to people in need and long-term solutions to global poverty. CARE provides millions of dollars in aid to 63 countries each year, offering programs in education, emergency relief, food security, health, economic development, and the environment.

Illness, child abuse and poverty are all sad facts of human life. The only effective way these and other problems can be addressed is through the permanent institutions that house the expertise and manage the resources necessary to meet human need. These institutions may serve local communities, such as Arlington Hospital or the Lombardi Center at Georgetown University, or they serve the nation and the world, like Childhelp, CARE, and the Salvation Army, but they all are necessary to the well-being and happiness of society. Yes, all are necessary and all need our ongoing help. For God's sake we can doing nothing less for "Our Lords the poor and the sick."

Rose with celebrity supporters of Childhelp USA in California, from left to right: Jack Scalia, Cheryl Ladd, Norm Crosby, Efrem Zimbalist, Jr., Carol Lawrence, Anne Jeffreys. Seated with Rose is Sophia Lee.

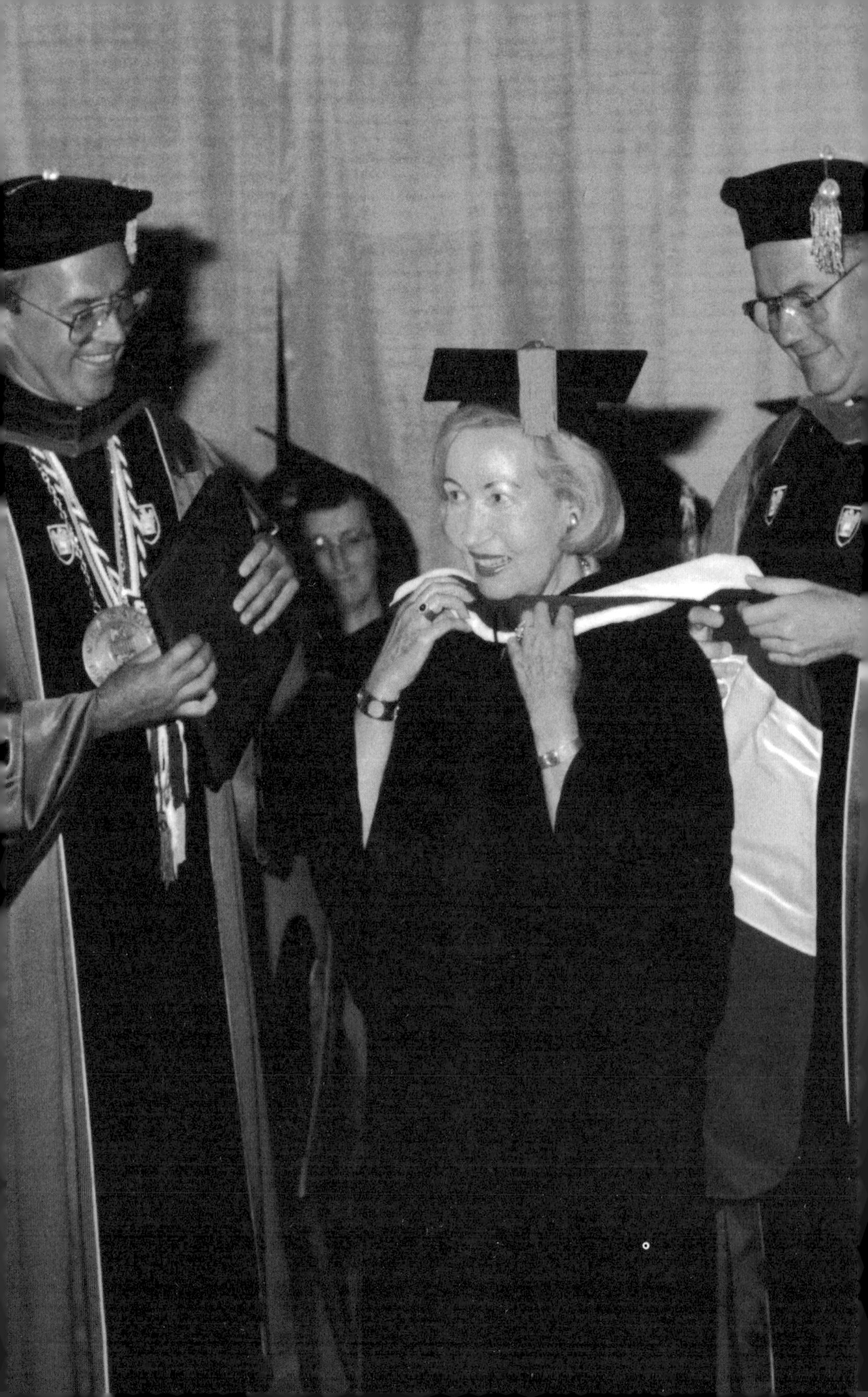

Chapter Nine

Support for Education

When you start your own business from nothing, you quickly learn how important education can be. Learning what you need to know from experience—from the daily necessities of management, marketing, and accounting—is fine, but it is so much easier to get a sound education first before stepping out into the world.

This precisely is what education means to me and why I support it—education provides the foundation for a successful life, not just in business affairs, but as a citizen, spouse, and friend. Knowledge is not just for so-called

Rose receives an honorary doctorate from Niagara University in 1986.

intellectuals—it is for all of us, because it enables us to become more and more human. The better we know who we are, the better we can help each other.

Thus over the years I have become deeply involved with several educational institutions, some Catholic, some not. My closest ongoing association is with a Catholic institution in my own community of Arlington, Virginia—Marymount University. Marymount was founded in 1950 by the Religious of the Sacred Heart of Mary, RSHM. The RSHMs have a 150-year tradition of ministry through education across four continents beginning in Beziers, France, in 1849. Various schools bearing the name "Marymount" are located in California, New York, Virginia, England, France, Italy, and Mexico.

The first American "Marymount" was founded in 1907 on the Hudson River in Tarrytown, New York, by Mother Joseph Butler. Marymount in Virginia was created at the suggestion of Bishop Peter L. Ireton of Richmond and implemented by the hard work of Mother Gerard Phelan. Thirteen freshman entered the first year, with nine of them comprising the first graduating class in 1952. The university now serves approximately thirty-nine hundred men and women in thirty-seven undergraduate majors and twenty-three graduate degree programs through its main campus and satellite campuses.

Supporting this institution, located only a few minutes from my home, appealed to me for different reason.

With Chairman of the Board Carmelita H. Tracey (left), Rose receives an honorary doctorate at Marymount University from Sister Eymard, RSHM, Marymount's president, 1996.

First, and most importantly, is its strong Catholic identity. Marymount "affirms that the exploration of humanity's relationship to the Divine is an integral part of the academic work of the University...." Second, Marymount seeks to create a unique community of learning "in which all members of the University interact with one another and the with the larger community outside the University." Third, I was impressed by the success of its nursing program in training qualified and compassionate nurses for local hospitals. Finally, I have always had the total confidence in the leadership supplied by the sisters directing the operations of the university.

Sr. Majella Berg, RSHM, president of Marymount for thirty-three years and now chancellor, became a very close friend. She remembers meeting me at a bank dedication in Arlington where she talked to me about shopping at the Connecticut Avenue and Tyson's Corners "House of Fine Fabrics" locations. It was then I told her to ask for a 20 percent discount whenever she shopped there. She remembers recently making good use of the discount, even though she cheerfully admits having a limited wardrobe.

That chance encounter led to my post on the Marymount University board, a position I still hold. Sr. Majella remembers that at the time the university's officials were excited for me to come on the board because successful businesswomen, who were rare then, were good role models for the women in the student body. (The first male students were not admitted until 1972!) Sr. Majella also recalls that I was not shy about challenging other board members with matching donations.

In addition to the endowed scholarship program for nurses, I helped to provide a new reception room just outside the library and lecture hall to entertain visiting guests and speakers. And, under the leadership of president Sr. Eymard Gallagher, RSHM, I am proud to have donated the funds for a new building, the Rose Benté Lee Student Center; when it is finished, the Student Center will house a gymnasium seating one thousand people, a pool with four hundred spectator seats, an all-night store, a café, an exercise room, and lounges in which students can relax, visit, and study. This center has long been needed on the campus, and I know it will only add to the strong sense of community already apparent there. I am thrilled that this Student Center will become the heart of a campus I have supported for so long.

Marymount University has just turned fifty years old, and has come a very long way since it was founded on the seventeen acres and four buildings owned by Admiral Presley M. Rixey, who was surgeon general to President Theodore Roosevelt. I am proud to be a trustee of Marymount University. But I have learned that sitting on a board of trustees is not merely window dressing, but is rather an immense responsibility. It is a community trust, and as such comes with a set of responsibilities and a level of accountability to see that the organization is well-managed and "on mission."

Most importantly, you have to know what skills are appropriate to bring to the table, and when it is time to speak and time to remain silent. It is important to clearly define the position, understanding what you can and cannot do, and what you should or should not do. It is vital that, in the exercise of your duties, you impart a positive set of institutional values, guiding the institution wisely, helping to establish purpose and place. Finally, you must use the boardroom and the corporate structure to craft a larger sense of community, what some have called a "culture of character," a culture prizing personal responsibility and community service.

I also had the privilege of serving on the Advisory Board of the University of Notre Dame for three years.

Notre Dame, of course, is the premiere Catholic institution of higher education in the United States. In the heartland of Indiana, Notre Dame was founded in 1842 by the Congregation of the Holy Cross and over the years has developed a national and international following of Catholics who regard it as a symbol of Catholic educational excellence.

Today the University of Notre Dame is home to more than ten thousand students studying all the academic specialties, on both the undergraduate and graduate level. Its mission statement reads, "Notre Dame's character as a Catholic academic community presupposes that no genuine search for truth in the human or cosmic order is alien to the life of faith...In all dimensions of the University, Notre Dame pursues its objectives through the formation of an authentic human community graced by the spirit of Christ."

As I have said, Bob Lee received an honorary doctorate from Notre Dame and often lectured there on the latest developments in communications. Fr. Theodore Hesburg and Fr. Ned Joyce asked Bob to consider establishing a telecommunications institute at the university, but they gave up on the idea when they figured out the endowment cost. Bob's close ties to Notre Dame led later to my own involvement as a member of the Notre Dame Advisory Board and supporter of the communications scholarship program.

Rose with Sister Gerard Majella, RSHM, past president and now provost of Marymount University, after receiving the Mother Gerard Phelan Gold Medal.

I became involved with another Catholic institution, Niagara University, through the insistence of an alumnus and old friend, the late Jim Keenan, who asked me to consider supporting his alma mater. Jim loved Niagara passionately and was always recalling his classes in metaphysics and lamenting the fact that this topic was so rarely taught any longer. But Jim assured me that Niagara University, located nearby the famed Niagara Falls in upstate New York, still had a very solid Catholic character and strong core curriculum.

Niagara University was founded in 1856 by the Vin-centian Fathers. Niagara now teaches more than twenty-three undergraduates, but keeps its average class size at only twenty-two and student-teacher ratio at 15 to 1. It has a particularly fine and beautiful library—Our Lady of Angels, with more than three hundred thousand volumes. Its president, Rev. Paul L. Golden, C.M., describes the university as having the spirit of St. Vincent de Paul, the patron saint of charitable giving, manifested in its many service-learning opportunities whereby the talents and energies of the students are put in service of the poor and less fortunate. The outward-looking mission of Niagara, like that of Marymount and other organizations I have served, appealed to me very much. The purpose of education, like the purpose of financial success, has to go beyond individual satisfaction.

This is lesson we learn over and over in life—even as a philanthropist and board member of various organizations, individual ambitions have to take second place to institutional ambitions. Success should be measured in institutional terms, not being in the spotlight.

Not all of my support for education has gone to Catholic schools. I recently helped to provide a one hundred-acre site for the Germanna Community College Educational Foundation in Culpeper, Virginia. Several donors got together on this project because we wanted to give this important community college in rural Virginia the means to establish a Technology Center. This project was instigated by the college in response to a joint resolution of the Virginia House of Delegates to select "a rural region of the state to provide of model center" for training in technology. This new center will help prepare the work force for heightened demand in technology skills, leading to greater employment in this less-developed part of Virginia.

This donation ended up becoming the single largest gift ever given to the College Foundation. The best part of this project was that we enabled the college to improve the quality of vocational education in an undeveloped part of Virginia. The real reward for me is always seeing people's lives changed—the real worth of our financial resources can be counted in the smiling faces of healthy children and confident young adults graduating from college knowing they are fully prepared for their first full-time job.

The Germanna Community College is one of twenty-three colleges in the Virginia Community College System.

Germanna is a community-based institution of higher education, based in Locust Grove, serving the counties of Caroline, Culpeper, King George, Madison, Orange, Spotsylvania, and Stafford and the City of Fredericksburg. It offers twelve majors and nine certificate programs as well as professional development classes.

The root word of "education" means "to build up." What is it that our schools, colleges, and universities build up? The aim must primarily be individual character. Character is the most important determining factor in our culture. As the psychologist William James once said, "Sow an act, reap a habit; sow a habit, reap a character; sow a character, reap a destiny." A culture that invests in the character of its citizens will reap a bright future, and that investment begins with children and education. I have made this the guiding principle of my philanthropy.

According to the *Oxford English Dictionary*, when Aristotle first used this term twenty-five hundred years ago, linking it with the consistent practice of virtuous actions, character meant "an instrument for marking and graving, impress, stamp, distinctive mark, distinctive nature." Character was the foundation for a successful life. For me, character still has this meaning. Each of us has a given set of possibilities, different actions we can undertake, opportunities we can use, and various roads we can travel.

Our character will determine whether we have the wisdom to choose the correct path and the courage to overcome its obstacles.

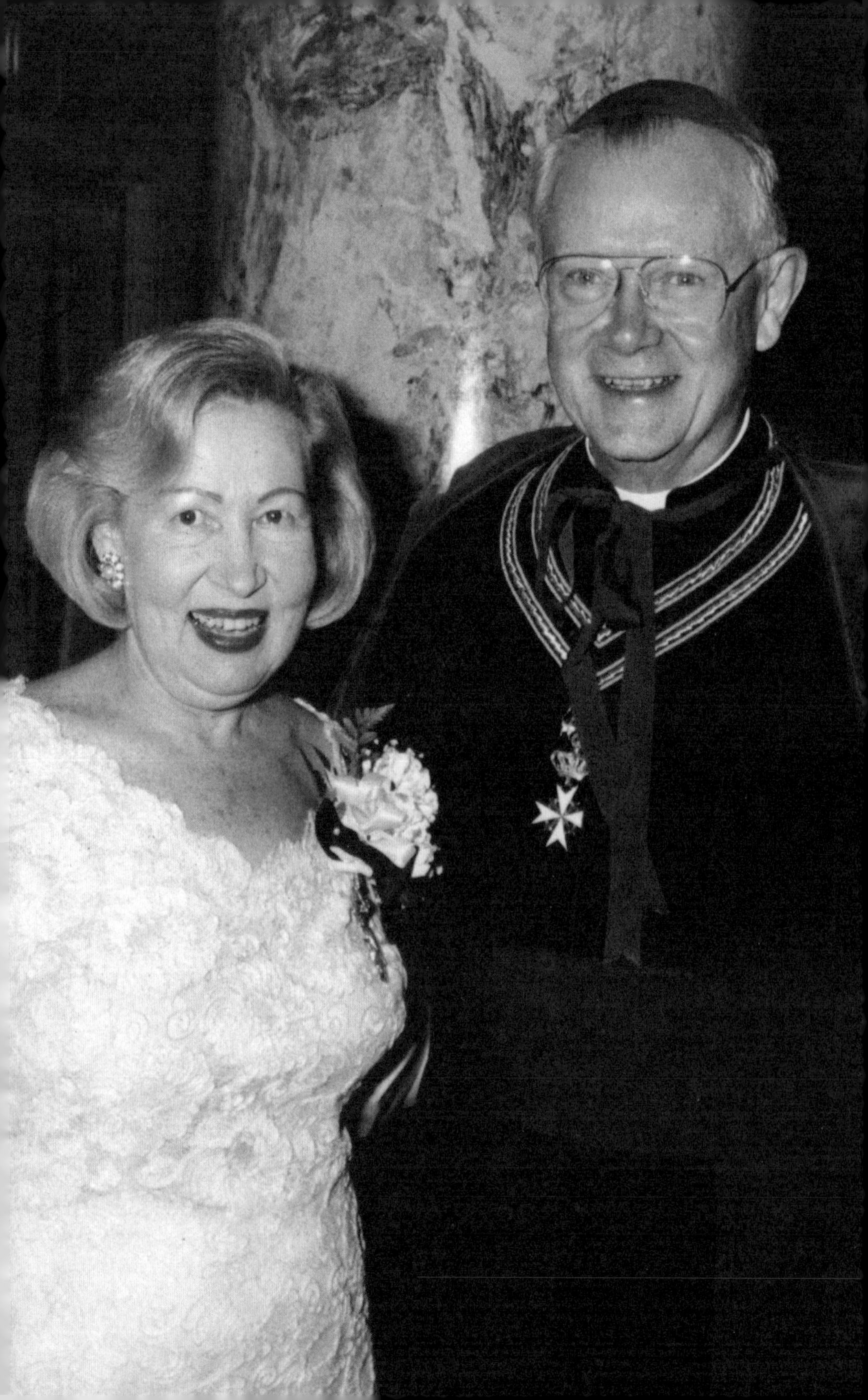

Chapter Ten

Giving Back to the Church

My faith in the Catholic Church has sustained my life and taught me that it is "better to give than to receive." Yes, I have received much, but what I have received from God I can never pay back to Him. I can only give back through the ministries of His Church. The Scripture tells us that when we give to the "least of these" we are giving directly to Christ.

This desire to give back has been with me since my religious upbringing in Fulda; it has been with me since my priest and my teacher gave me lessons to explain my faith.

Rose with James Cardinal Hickey of Washington, D.C. in 1987.

Giving in the spirit of gratitude is all any of us can do—everyone in his or her own way has taken a risky journey, as I did when I crossed the Atlantic Ocean to a new land.

In that journey many of us have received the solace of an ancient faith, as I did when, speaking very little English, I attended the Latin Mass at St. Matthew's Cathedral in downtown Washington. Faith sustained me through the loss of Ray and Bob and throughout my business and philanthropic career. God indeed has been good to me and continues to be, to this very day.

The Church, as it is said, contains "many mansions"—this is especially true of the many opportunities we are given to help her apostolates. From her schools and colleges, orders and institutes, hospitals and charities, the Church has been trying to meet human needs over the whole world for two thousand years. I am grateful to have been part of many organizations that represent this worldwide effort to express the love of God toward those who need Him most.

In 1987 I was thrilled to become a "Dame of Malta"—the investiture was one of the most important events in my life.

The Sovereign Military Hospitallier Order of St. John of Jerusalem of Rhodes and of Malta, commonly known as the Order of Malta, traces its origins to Jerusalem in 1099.

It was founded by Blessed Gerard when the Holy City was recovered by the Christians. It is the fourth oldest religious order in Christendom, next to the Basilians, the Augustinians, and the Benedictines.

Blessed Gerard founded a hospice-infirmary for pilgrims in Jerusalem. The order constructed great fortresses at vulnerable points in the Kingdom of Jerusalem and launched its own military campaigns in the defense of Christendom. The order also expanded along important routes of travel its network of hospices for the care, service, and defense of pilgrims.

The order was driven from the Holy Land by the Muslims and was headquarted first in Cyprus then in Rhodes. In 1522 the order left Rhodes to escape Muslim attack and settled on the island of Malta, where it successfully defeated the much larger force of Muslims in 1565. The Order of Malta, thus, can be accurately credited with keeping the whole of Christendom from falling to Muslim rule.

Although the Order of Malta no longer maintains its military status, today its mission is still to protect and serve the needs of the poor and the sick all over the world. The rule is still the same as it has been for five centuries, centered on the helping "Our Lords the poor and the sick."

In addition to all the good works of the order, I felt that there was a need for the Knights of Malta to look after the growing needs of older Americans. So I donated the funds to construct a permanent facility of thirty-two units to care for the frail elderly while the Archdiocese of Washington provided thirty acres of land in Hyattsville, Maryland.

Malta House, as it is now called, was dedicated in the fall of 1995; it is an assisted-living arrangement in which the elderly, no longer able to care for themselves, can continue a humane, dignified way of life. For those who have come to live there, Malta House has been the answer to periods of anguished searching, prayers, and doubts about what to do when a parent begins to need more attention than sons, daughters, friends, or home health-care personnel can provide.

These days, with the advent of mass transportation and upward mobility, the extended family is no longer the norm. Families are not always in a position to care for an older relative or friend who needs special diets and exercise, sophisticated medical care and technology, and access to the latest drugs. No generation in history has faced the new problems associated with longevity. Out of necessity we turn to health-care professionals to assist our elderly relatives. Malta House provides this care in an environment of dignity and comfort. Obviously a great advantage of this facility is the constant presence of a Catholic priest and a chapel for religious service—these services are held in the Rose Benté Lee Chapel, named in honor of my gift. I wanted to make sure that Malta House felt like a comfortable home, not a sterile hospital environment. In addi-

Rose with Mike Miskovsky (left), Christopher Dorment (2nd from left), and Cardinal Hickey at the opening of Malta House in 1995.

tion to the chapel, Malta House has a wellness center, library, and an activities program featuring musical performances by professional soloists and groups.

Through the Friendly Visitor Program, volunteer visitors come and spend time with the residents, arrange holiday parties, assist residents with tasks, and accompany them on walks or other small excursions. The Knights and Dames of Malta, through their extensive volunteer program, make sure that this and other programs are fully staffed throughout the year.

Malta House, like the oncology clinic named after Bob at Arlington Hospital, treats each person as a separate individual with a unique personality and desires. This is a distinctive difference that can be experienced at Malta House at any time. At Malta House, residents live in a community, not a ward. They have both privacy and the social interaction they need to remain alert and happy. People look out for each other, and the fear of isolation is shattered by the warm sense of community.

These are the words I spoke on a sunny day in October 1995 as we dedicated Malta House:

> *Your Eminence, Mr. President, esteemed officers, Knights and Dames of Malta, and honored guests: Today is a historic moment in the work of the Knights of Malta. We continue a legacy of caring for the sick and needy begun by this organization nearly one thousand years ago.*
>
> *I am both privileged and humbled to be a part of this meaningful dedication.*
>
> *As a little girl in Germany, I never imagined that I would one day have the honor of becoming a Dame of Malta. But I had that honor because of God's love and the wonderful opportunities available in this great country of ours.*

As a result of God's gifts, I have grown to love and revere this order of the Vatican and its members, many of whom have become my dearest friends.

So I wanted to give something back. If my gift of Malta House brings recognition to the Order of the Knights of Malta and its international ministry of good works, then I will have succeeded in fulfilling a dream I long shared with someone I deeply loved.

In fact, none of this would have been possible, however, without the inspiration of my late, beloved husband, the Honorable Robert Emmet Lee, in whose memory we dedicate this facility. Bob joins us in spirit today. I know that he is smiling down from his heavenly vantage point, and saying, "Well, it finally happened!"

They say that good things are worth waiting for. In this case, Malta House is all we dreamed it might be—even more. I am so grateful to God for the opportunity to serve him and my fellow man by playing a small part in this wonderful moment.

My deepest appreciation and thanks to all who have worked so hard for so many years to make this dream a reality.

Thank you and God bless you.

There is another ancient order within the Church that I am proud to have been associated with as a "Lady of the Order"—the Equestrian Order of the Holy Sepulchre of

Jerusalem. This order has a special glory of its own, the honor and distinction of having been chosen to guard the Tomb of Christ.

The Order of the Holy Sepulchre goes back to the first Knights, which was established by Godfrey de Bouillon around the Sepulchre of Our Lord as a guard of honor immediately after the conquest of Jerusalem in 1099. They were approved as an Order by a Bull of Approbation by Pope Pascal II in February 1113.

With the fall of the Latin Kingdom of Jerusalem, the Knights of the Holy Sepulchre were driven out of Palestine. They then went to Italy and lived the lives of religious Knights, maintaining a religious rule of life with all its duties. Priories and monasteries of the order were established in France, Spain, Poland, Belgium, and Italy.

Pope Leo XIII authorized, for the first time, the conferring of honors of the order upon women, who were to be styled "Ladies of the Holy Sepulchre" and would share in all the rights and privileges of the Knights.

The objective of the order is to revive, in modern form, the spirit and ideals of the Crusades with the weapon of the faith, the apostolate, and Christian charity. More specifically, the purpose consists in the preservation and propagation of the faith in the Holy Land; assistance to and development of the missions of the Latin as well as the Oriental rites; providing for its charitable, cultural, and social undertakings; and the defense

Rose wtih Cardinal Hickey at the investiture into the Knights of the Holy Sepulchre in 1987.

of the rights of the Catholic Church in the Holy Land, the cradle of the order.

Therefore, the Knights sponsor an important non-profit organization called the Holy Land Foundation, which I have supported, that actively helps the needy, the disadvantaged, and those who suffer great hardships around the world.

The government of the order is entrusted by the Holy Father himself. Thus the protection of the Holy See is rendered more powerful, and brings about official recognition by the whole Christian world of the order.

Another marvelous order within the Church is the Daughters of Charity, which started its work in Haiti at the Cité Soleil with the founding of "Our Lady of Providence" convent in 1975.

The Cité Soleil is a swampy area located in the northwest of Port-au-Prince, with a population of about 250,000. The majority of the people are illiterate, living in homes made of cardboard, sticks, and boards. There is a very high infant mortality rate mainly due to lack of proper nutrition. Once I was made aware by friends that their nutrition center was about to be shut down, I assisted in providing the resources to keep it open. This would have been a tragedy leading to needless suffering, especially among the children, and much loss of life.

I also served on a committee that supported the infrastructure at Cité Soleil, including its programs in health, nutrition, and education; immunization and other medical care; cooking; sewing; reading; and crafts. All this is made available to parents while their undernourished children are nursed back to health by the sisters.

The Daughters of Charity were founded by St. Vincent in 1617 in France. They were originally comprised of women from relatively modest backgrounds who wished to devote themselves to the service of the poor and the sick in their individual villages and parishes. As time progressed, ladies of the nobility and upper-middle class joined in these efforts. Although their contributions were different, the wealthy and modest worked side by side in helping the poor.

In 1630, Msgr. Vincent was joined by Louise de Marillac, who began assisting him in the organization and visitation of the charities. Louise de Marillac desired to bring each of the charities together, as they were dispersed throughout Paris. She hoped that she could give them a better formation and accompany them in their corporal services as well as spiritual.

Under the authorization of Msgr. Vincent, she received the first six Daughters into her home on November 29, 1663. This date marks the birth of the Company of the Daughters of Charity. The company was a novelty in the Church of that era, which did not permit religious women to leave their cloisters. Perhaps it was their boldness as women entering actively into the world that attracted me to their mission. Vincent recommended that the Daughters care for the poor in their homes so they could get to know each person individually and in their natural setting. He told the sisters to be good Christians first and to promise to serve God faithfully through their service to the poor.

The Daughters of Charity are not religious nuns in a strict canonical sense. They are consecrated to Jesus for the service of the poor by private, annual vows of poverty, chastity, obedience, and service. "The principal end to which God has called and established the Daughters of Charity is to honor our Lord Jesus Christ as the source and model of all charity, serving him corporally and spiritually in the person of the poor," said St. Vincent.

Today, the Daughters of Charity are present in five continents, divided into eighty-one provinces and regions. According to the wishes of their founders, priority is always given to the most needy. Their work at the Cité Soleil amidst the crushing poverty of Haiti, exemplifies a spirit that is impossible to resist.

Of course, the needy are found everywhere, even in your own neighborhood. I have done whatever I can to help the community of Northern Virginia. One way has been to support Catholic Charities of the Diocese of Arlington. Catholic Charities, a national organization found in every Catholic diocese in the United States, is a nonprofit social service agency dedicated to implementing the Church's social mission to aid needy families, individuals, and communities. Catholic Charities provides a full gamut of social services for children, the elderly, prisoners, the disabled, the emotionally disturbed, and those facing extreme emergencies.

This organization represents the Church's work as a mediating institution in society, standing between those state agencies empowered to help the needy and the faithful in local communities who want to participate directly in corporal works of mercy. Catholic Charities is the central pipeline for the Church to deliver her resources to the people who need them.

There are hundreds of Catholic organizations across this country and around the world that help the needy.

Rose at Malta House.

There are two more I would like to mention briefly, the Little Sisters of the Poor in Richmond, Virginia, and the Missionaries of Charity, founded by Mother Teresa of Calcutta, whose shelter in New Jersey I have long been associated with.

We can hardly do enough for these religious, both nuns and priests, who have given their lives in service to Christ and His Church. With this in mind, I have participated gladly in the yearly gala to raise money for SOAR, an organization that supports retired Catholic sisters.

Over the years I have come to appreciate the importance of like-minded people coming together voluntarily to collaborate in keeping the community strong. One such organization I have supported is the John Carroll Society of Washington. Based at St. Patrick's Church, the Society was founded in 1951 to support the Archbishop of Washington in his various ministries and oversight of the Archdiocese. Its members are drawn from all areas of professional and business life in the Washington area.

Named after the first Catholic bishop in the United States, Bishop John Carroll, the Society organizes the annual Red Mass prior to the opening of the U.S. Supreme Court's judicial year, on the Sunday before the first Monday in October; the annual Red Mass for health-care professionals on the Fourth Sunday of Lent; and St. Nicolas Day Mass for children.

The Knights of Malta, the Daughters of Charity, the Knights of the Holy Sepulchre, Catholic Charities, the John Carroll Society—these have all proved worthy means of helping to build the Body of Christ. I am proud to have been associated with all of them. Each of them embodies the readiness to help and the virtue of compassion that Christ demands of everyone.

In my files I have kept a poem, entitled "Unawares" that expresses my deepest convictions why each of us must respond to the needy at our doorstep. It is easier than we think to be caught "unawares" and fail to return the love that Christ has so freely bestowed upon us:

Unawares

They said, "The Master is coming to honor the town today,
And none can tell at what house or home the Master will choose to stay."
And I thought while my heart beat wildly, what if he should come to mine,
How would I strive to entertain and honor the Guest Divine!

And straight I turned to toiling, to make my home more neat;
I swept, and polished and garnished, and decked it with blossoms sweet.
I was troubled for fear the Master, might come ere my work was done
And I hasted and worked the faster, and watched the hurrying sun.

But right in the midst of my duties a woman came to my door;
She had come to tell her sorrows and my comfort an aid to implore,
And I said, "I cannot listen, nor help you any, today;
I have greater things to attend to," and the pleader turned away.

But soon there came another—a cripple, thin pale and gray—
And said: "Oh, let me stop and rest a while in your house, I pray!
I have traveled far since morning, I am hungry and faint and weak;
My heart is full of misery, and comfort and help I seek."

And I cried, "I am grieved and sorry, but I cannot help you today.
I look for a great and noble Guest," and the cripple went away;
And the day wore onward swiftly—and my task was nearly done,
And a prayer was ever in my heart that the Master to me might come.

And I thought I would spring to meet Him, and serve Him with utmost care,
When a little child stood near me with a face so sweet and fair—
Sweet, but with marks of teardrops—and his clothes were tattered and old;
A finger was bruised and bleeding, and his little feet were cold.

And I said, "I'm sorry for you—you are sorely in need of care;
But I cannot stop to give it, you must hasten otherwhere."
And at the words, a shadow swept o'er his blue-veined brow—
"Someone will feed and clothe you, dear, but I am too busy now."

At last the day was ended, and my toil was over and done;
My house was swept and garnished—and I watched in the dark—alone.
Watched—but no footfall sounded, no one paused at my gate;
No one entered my cottage door; I could only pray—and wait.

I waited till night had deepened, and the Master had not come.
"He has entered some other door," I said, "And gladdened some other home!
My labor has been for nothing," and I bowed my head and I wept,
My heart was sore with longing—yet—in spite of it all—I slept.

Then the Master stood before me, and his face was grave and fair;
"Three times today I came to your door, and I craved your pity and care;
Three times you sent me onward, unhelped and uncomforted;
And the blessing you might have had was lost and your chance to serve has fled."

Rose with James Belson (center) and Robert Flanagan (right) receives the Cross Pro Merito Melitensi from the Knights of Malta in 1993.

*"O Lord, dear Lord, forgive me! How could I know it was Thee?"
My very soul was shamed and bowed in the depths of humility,
And he said, "The sin is pardoned, but the blessing is lost to thee;
For, comforting not the least of Mine, you have failed to comfort Me."*

This poem reminds us of a simple truth that is so easy to forget—the opportunity of serving our Lord is always at hand, it is as close as a neighbor, or a stranger, in need. While we are busily making sure that all the trappings of success are clearly visible to everyone around us, we risk missing the deeper purpose of all we own—it came from God, belongs to Him, and can be used in His service. None of us want to leave this life having lived "unawares."

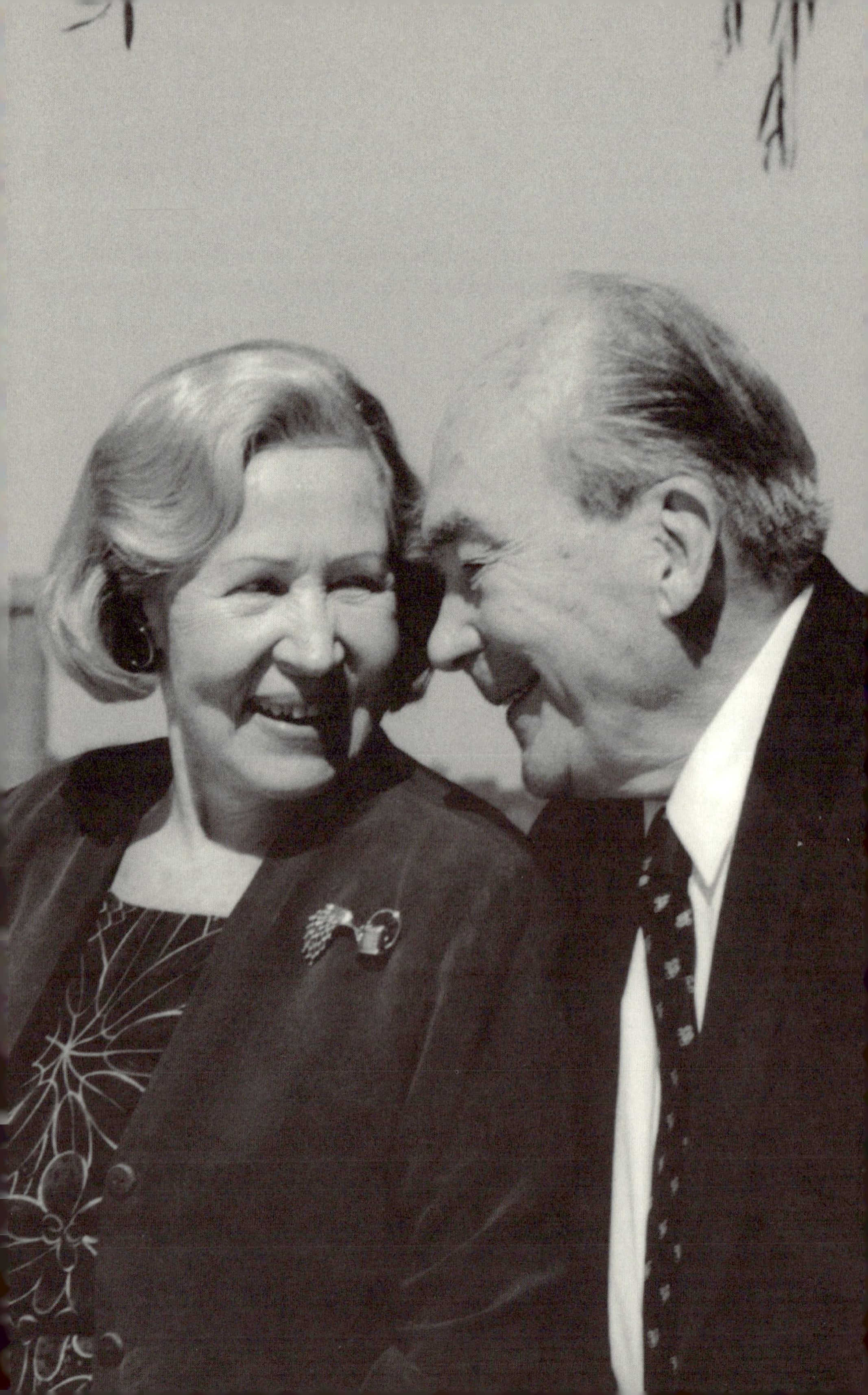

Chapter Eleven

Lessons from Life

Mark Twain has a famous saying to the effect that the older he grew, the smarter his parents seemed to become. This remark is more pertinent now than ever. Never has there been a generation of young people who seemed more impatient with the advice of their elders.

Yes, the older generation always seems to lament the foolishness of the younger generation. Perhaps much of the criticism has been exaggerated by those of us who have forgotten our own youthful rebellion.

Rose and Bill Ostapenko on the terrace of the Kennedy Center, Fall 1999

But something unusual has happened to the current generation of young people—they have extraordinarily high expectations for success and financial prosperity. With a growing economy and the need for well-trained employees in entry-level jobs, it is not difficult for someone to land a lucrative job fresh out of college.

Once they start their jobs, however, they often expect rapid advancement and big salaries in a short period of time. If the payoff does not come, they often quickly exit the company that trained them and look for the pot of gold at the end of another rainbow. This is a generation of individuals bred to look out for themselves above all; they know little about loyalty and even less about focusing on long-term goals.

It is a hard world, they will say, and you have to look out for yourself. I agree, but looking out only for yourself does not make life any easier or the world any better. Such self-centeredness takes away not only from your character but from your capacity for good management and leadership.

When asked how I was able to get the best effort from those who worked for me at my business, I say that employers must lead by example: Show your staff how hard you work and they will very likely do the same. I once had a cleaning woman who did not want to clean the bathrooms, so I said 'Give me the sponge, I do not mind doing it,' I think that left an impression! I never asked anyone to do a job that I would not do myself.

Starting a business from scratch gave me the opportunity to learn good working habits. You cannot watch the clock; your cannot worry about working only eight hours a day, you have to work as long as it takes, even at night and on weekends. Ray and I used to work many days from 6 a.m. to 11 p.m. We used to do all the work ourselves, saving money by building all our own shelving and display cabinets.

We also learned to keep our money in the business; we reinvested everything to keep the business growing. Taking money out of the business for short-term rewards is a temptation to avoid. It takes time to build something of value, something that will last and outlive the competition.

I always kept my eye on the competition. When I got concerned, or a little bit scared, I just redoubled my effort at being the best, at offering the finest merchandise, service, and price in the area. I made sure that my sales personnel looked good, smiled at customers, and acted in a pleasing manner (qualities all too rare these days!). The customers truly are always right, and when you treat them that way, they will come back and give you their loyalty.

The main lesson I have learned is to never give up on yourself or others. Rely on your faith in God, your capacity for hard work and self-control, to make what you need for yourself and for others in society who need your help. These are simple lessons, but lessons that need to be rediscovered in this country—lessons that if once again taken seriously will help to renew the character of the nation.

I have often been asked if I am a success. I answer, "Yes." But I do not think of my success in purely financial terms. My real success has been in helping others through my business and through my investments in effective charities that will go on doing good works after I am gone. But on my watch, I can honestly say that I did my part to keep them going.

I always wanted to be a success like my brothers and like Ray, my first husband. Being my own boss helped to keep me motivated—no one was going to do it for me. I could rise to my own level of accomplishment. I did not have to fit into someone else's strategic plan. I would either make my own success or be the author of my own failure.

But I was lucky and I was blessed. I was blessed to meet Ray and Bob. I hope they were blessed to meet me as well. Ray and I made a good business team, and our talents complemented one another. He helped me to become a businesswoman by leaving the Singer Sewing Machine Co. and opening the "The House of Fine Fabrics." Bob and I were a great pair both socially and culturally. Bob brought me into the wider world of government and diplomacy. After so many years of keeping my nose to the proverbial grindstone, he helped me to laugh and enjoy life. His Irish humor tempered my

German seriousness. I miss both Ray and Bob very much, but I know that they are with God, helping to guide me in my current life and work.

God has truly been good to me; He has helped me again and again. Every good decision I have attributed to the influence of the Holy Spirit. God has helped to keep me from being preoccupied with myself and my own problems.

I also believe that I have been fortunate to be part of some of our country's greatest institutions: Marymount University, Childhelp USA, the Knights of Malta and Malta House, the Equestrian Order of the Holy Sepulchre, the Kennedy Center, and so many other organizations that represent our finest efforts to create a good and loving country. I firmly believe that our organizations influence our lives and our values, and these organizations are positive influences on the lives of those they touch.

All of us must continue to work through organizations like these to make our country better, stronger, safer, healthier, and more compassionate. I worry that we are so divided and fractured that we are losing the ability to work together in common cause. We are a good people in a great country, but we are constantly tempted by the ideal of rugged individualism. Our lives can be richer, nobler, and better if we learn to give of ourselves—to give back to our communities.

I know that some people may say, "Well, Rose, easy for you to say. You've made it. You are in retirement and life is good. It is not so easy for the rest of us." I understand why someone would think that. Some things are easier for me. But I started with nothing, in a foreign country, knowing only a few people and working in a sewing center. It would be hard to find a more humble beginning. But hard work, attention to detail, investing back in the company, hiring good people, finding a quality product, building a good relationship with customers, carefully expanding the business, and giving back to the community in retirement were all decisions I made. I can only wish that others will experience that joy of giving back that has made my life complete.

But I know that the decisions, made one at a time, add up. Our lives are the sum products of our decisions, especially the decisions we make in response to tragedy and unforeseen setbacks. I know that we can make our lives into something greater and more rewarding if we can see past the short-term payoffs, keep an abiding faith in God, and continue to care about those who have little opportunity to live full and happy lives.

I know that our people, with only a little help and support, can accomplish amazing feats. I remember only too well what I was able to accomplish with the support of my family and the money for a ticket across the Atlantic from my brother Leo.

The culture of the United States influences the entire world. More and more societies around the globe are feel-

Rose sitting in her sculpture gallery at the National Museum for Women in the Arts.

Rose Benté Lee 177

ing the direct influence of American lifestyles through the media, the Internet, and the export of our technology. This is a time of monumental possibilities for doing good or for doing ill. The question remains: Will we be examples to the world of hard work and giving to others, or will we fulfill the stereotypes as greedy, materialistic Westerners who only know how to take from others for their own profit?

America has been great because its roots were formed in devout Christian soil and nourished by the daily practice of prayer, hard work, and sacrifice. To continue this legacy requires that we never forget the lessons of our success, both as individuals and as a community. In this book, I have tried to show how the American Dream, bolstered by both the faith and character of this nation, has been fulfilled in my life. And I am only one among millions who can tell this story.

We have come now to what some people might call the end of the story and the end of this book. But it is not the end of the story, even though it is the end of the book. This book ends with another beginning, a new beginning of my life with a wonderful and unforeseen blessing, a man named Bill.

Early in 1998, my pastor, Fr. James Gould of St. Agnes Parish Church, called and asked me if I would like a man to call me—his name was William Ostapenko. Fr. Gould said he had known him for six years, since the death of

Bill's wife in 1993. I was not interested in dating at the time, but I reluctantly said it was "OK" for him to call. Bill called me right away and asked if we could get together. I looked at my calendar and suggested a week or so later at 5 p.m. in the afternoon. Bill, to my surprise, said he would be over in ten minutes (he lived close by). He arrived and we sat in the living room. When Bill explained that he was only interested in making a friend, I was relieved and decided to like him.

Bill and I had our first real date at the Cosmos Club in Washington a week later. On the second date, a week after that, he popped the question. I could not believe he said it. He seemed a little overly excited. But eventually I said "yes" because he was a good man, good company, and possessed a deep Catholic faith. We also shared many interests, especially music and opera. Bill happened to be an accomplished pianist and violinist.

Bill had lived a very interesting and successful life before I met him. William Ostapenko served in the United States Navy for twenty-eight years, achieving the rank of Rear Admiral, before working in aircraft engineering for General Motors and the General Electric Co. He came to Washington and worked fifteen years with the U.S. Department of Transportation as a chief engineer, and eventually founded an engineering consulting firm.

We were married on August 14, 1999 at St. Agnes by Fr. Gould. My niece and nephew were present, and we were all pleasantly surprised by the arrival of my two stepsons, Bob Lee's two sons, Robert and Michael. They came and stood with us at the altar while we shared our vows and celebrated the nuptial Mass. Bill and I immediately left for five days at the Greenbriar Resort in West Virginia. After seven years of being single, I was once again sharing my life with a wonderful man. Not only do I never give up, it is clear that God never gives up on me. Perhaps that is the greatest lesson of all: Behind the scenes of all we do there is a Presence watching us "unawares," watching to pick us up when we stumble, dry our tears when we cry, and find us a friend when we feel lonely. All this help will be ours, if are willing to receive it—yes, to receive Him.

Our wedding celebration, Bill's and mine, continues. We have many wonderful, caring friends who from time to time, invite us to their homes and surprise us with the most pleasant dinner party celebrations in honor of our marriage. One such recently was hosted by our friends, Colonel and Mrs. Joseph Brown. Theresa Brown gave a most happy toast to me which I would like to repeat here, at the closing of my book. It is as follows:

A Toast to the Bride, Rose Ann Lee!

by Theresa Brown

Rose Ann, Rose Ann, Rose Ann all alone.
You could tell she was lonely when she answered the phone

She worked, she volunteered, she travelled the globe.
But when she came home there was just ONE in her abode!

She needed a man—strong, tall, and wise,
But none she met would turn her eyes.

We saw her in Springtime, in gay Paree!
We watched her in Venice in a gondola by the sea.
She danced 'neath the stars on the Royal Viking Sun,
But not ONE guy her heart had won.

She smiled in Sydney when she heard the Aussies speak.
She dined with the Bedouins in Sharm El Sheikh.
She conversed with Romanovs in St. Petersburg so fine.
She admired the jewels in Dresden and the castles on the Rhine.

But nary a man measured up to her ideal.
Until one day the Admiral, a man named Bill
came along, swept her off her feet and stole her heart.
And a wedding in summer gave Rose Ann a fresh start.

Now they're a pair—hold your glasses to Rose and Bill.
Let's toast their happiness and to all their dreams fulfilled!

*Rose and her husband William Ostapenko
a few months after their marriage.*

Rose Benté Lee   183

Appendix I—List of Philanthropies

(alphabetical order)

This is a list of the philanthropies receiving major support from Rose Benté Lee.

Arlington Hospital
Catholic Charities of Northern Virginia
Childhelp USA
Daughters of Charity/Cité Soleil (Haiti)
Equestrian Order of the Holy Sepulchre
Smithsonian Institution ("First Ladies")
Germana Community College
Hospice of Northern Virginia
John F. Kennedy Center for the Performing Arts
Knights of Malta
Vincent Lombardi Cancer Center-Georgetown Unv. Hospital
Marymount University (Arlington, VA)
National Museum of Women in the Arts
National Symphony Orchestra
Niagara University
University of Notre Dame
Washington Opera
Jewish Council for the Aging
United Jewish Appeal Foundation

Appendix 2—Honors and Awards

1986: Doctor of Humane Letters, Niagara University

1987: Investiture, the Sovereign Order of the Knights of Malta

1988: Gold Medal, The University of Notre Dame

1993: Cross Pro Merito Melitensi, Knights of Malta

1995: Investiture, Equestrian Order of the Holy Sepulchre

1996: Doctor of Humane Letters, Marymount University

1997: Mother Gerard Phelan Gold Medal, Marymount University

ODE TO MY LIEBCHEN
R·O·S·E A·N·N

Some years ago
a trauma came
into my long existence
I found myself alone and sad
devoid of any interests.

I plunged into this new wide world
and somehow found it different
The social whirl and all the girls
so interested in tradition.

And then one day I met a girl
who made my old pulse quicken
I quickly tied her down and then
we had a great vacation.

My love for her is nurtured
she is the sweetest lady
Each day that passes
makes me think, my God
must really love me.

At times I am indeed
depressed, and life seems not
worth living
But then I see her smile at me
black clouds are disappearing.

And so I count each day a plus
when her I am enjoying
But dread the day when God must say
its time you must be leaving.

And it will come and I will say,
farewell my little liebling
Don't cry for me since I shall be
awaiting our reunion.

But you, my dear, may shed
one tear for this old goat
who loves you — until the
day you pass away and we
shall be united.

But wait, there's something missing
Where is Ray, and where is
Rex? Well, they'll have
to get together. There
is simply nothing
left

Robert E. Lee   September 27, 1985

186   *An American Dream*